D1567344

IMPROVISATION IN MUSIC

IMPROVISATION IN MUSIC

Ways Toward Capturing Musical Ideas
and Developing Them

BY

GERTRUDE PRICE WOLLNER

BOSTON
BRUCE HUMPHRIES
PUBLISHERS

ACKNOWLEDGMENTS

First, to those friends, pupils, and associates who so patiently helped me to move from the state of improvised formulation to the seasoned and tested statements and final form of this book; especially Joan Nemser, Norma Fryatt, Evelyn Dow, Maurine Burgess, James Boujoukos, Ruth Seeger, Florence Cane, Elizabeth Delza, and to R.E.D.—inexpressible gratitude.

And my thanks particularly to Cyrus Rogers and Joseph Ascherl, among the many others of Doubleday, whose knowledge, talents, and humor often braced this musician-turned-author.

I think with deep gratitude of my inspired musician-teachers who gave so much more than technical skill and repertoire. Katherine Ruth Heyman, my first great artist-teacher, and then E. Robert Schmitz and Harold Samuel. In improvisation Dr. Frederick Schlieder's performance and teaching of the subject were unique and remarkable. Later, Dr. Ernest Ferand, the international authority in improvisation, was truly inspiring. His approach to figured bass for improvisation, along with the freer forms, opened many new vistas.

Hugo Kauder, master of strict counterpoint, arrived just as the need to search for the subtle balance between written composition and improvisation was greatest. Joseph Schillinger (to whom Gershwin went while working on *Porgy and Bess*) was extremely contributive in unusual ways.

Albert Stoessel revealed a world of conducting, orchestration, score-reading, oratorio, and performed my first major opus, for strings and percussion. And how can I express my esteem, my homage, to the distinguished French musician and teacher Mlle. Nadia Boulanger . . . her criticism sometimes sharp but always exalting!

I must not neglect to mention my first teacher in music pedagogy, Harriet Seymour, guiding young teachers through the maze of music material, toward finding the best. We soon began to realize that the longest and most difficult pieces were not necessarily the most important in a young teacher's repertoire, however proud one might be of concerto performances. We discovered the value of folk music and the need to improvise accompaniments to them. We played, with careful listening, Schumann, Schubert, early Bach, Bartók, and other masters who had composed much fine (and short!) music for their children and students.

With Melzar Chaffee came chamber music. Since then a lifetime joy. Pure ecstasy.

My thanks to Alys Bentley and the Dalcroze teachers who taught music students freedom of movement, rhythms, eurhythmics, modern dance, as a much-needed balance to our sitting crouched over a piano for hours at a time. Music as related to the dance made lasting and valuable impressions.

And finally, a late tribute to my father, who taught me the rare value of searching for the right teacher, finding the right specialist in music, as I needed to probe into a related subject. For my father, music was life, and my memory of his natural improvisations in many moods is extremely vivid.

Out of so many of these rich experiences my love of improvisation grows.

"I sit down, I start to play, to improvise, depending upon whether my soul is sad or gay, serious or playful. If I succeed in catching an idea, then my endeavor is directed to an elaboration of the work according to the rules of the art."   JOSEF HAYDN.

"When I was nine my parents gave me a piano mistress. I very quickly learned to read music, and as a result of reading, soon had a longing to improvise, a pursuit to which I devoted myself, and which for a long time was my favorite occupation. I was frequently reproached for wasting my time in that way instead of practising properly, but I was definitely of a different opinion, and the reproaches vexed me considerably. Although today I understand and admit the need of this discipline for a child of nine or ten, I must say that my constant work at improvisation was not absolutely fruitless; for on the one hand, it contributed to my better knowledge of the piano, and, on the other, it sowed the seed of music ideas."   IGOR STRAVINSKY, in *Autobiography*

"Making music extemporaneously has truly proven to be an ageless craft . . . the entire history of music shows the urge of composers and performers to improvise, to express themselves on the spur of the moment."   FREDERICK DORIAN, in *The Musical Workshop*

Contents

CHAPTER I

Invitation to Exciting Music-Making

IN ORDER to enter the exciting world of music improvisation, no passport in the way of a special gift is required.

Our time is seeing a revival of improvisation, and the teaching of improvisation has come to the fore. In the past, teaching methods in music have often been either stilted and stiff or loose and careless, but progress has been made toward an ideal of discipline and freedom. The aim in teaching improvisation is the attainment of fluency, discipline, and control.

From years of practical experience in teaching both adults and children, I can go further and assert that improvisation can even be self-taught. Of course, some direction is needed, and this book is intended to supply direction, but I can assure the reader that it has been demonstrated many times that self-teaching in improvisation can be successful.

How often have I heard, "Improvisation can't be taught. It's a talent. Unless you are born with this talent, you will never achieve the freedom of improvisation."

It is unfortunate if such misleading remarks have deterred any one from first attempts at extempore composition. Along with the fallacy that one must have a special talent to improvise, let us discard some other widely held misconceptions about improvisation. Improvisation is an *active,* not a *passive,* pursuit. It definitely is not a pleasant business of rambling over the piano keys while in a state of reverie. Nor is improvisation a matter of indulgence in drifting, vague moods, a dreamy escape from living. Nor, again, is it a makeshift, something purely fleeting that will never survive.

There is nothing passive about improvisation. On the contrary, the student is invited to enter a world of music-making in which the first thing he must learn is to face the unexpected without anxiety or nervousness. He is invited, not to drift idly, but to call upon his resourcefulness and power of quick decision. To express himself skillfully, the extempore composer must learn to gain control over his materials even while in a state of intense excitement. He must deal with themes that were strange to him the moment before. He must be on the alert. He must learn to solve his problems quickly. The extempore composer discovers the basic laws of improvisation and functions within them, but these laws permit a wide variety of free play and demand great flexibility.

The approach to improvisation may be called creative spontaneity. Improvisation, in fact, is the externalizing of a sudden flash within. The sound is captured for a second by the inner ear and then released through the swift action of fingers on a keyboard. The flash is so swift that notation on paper cannot keep up with it. The fingers can play faster than they can write music, though in the fusion of mind and emotion which occurs in the happiest phases of improvisation, much is not captured, even so, by the racing fingers.

Improvisation then is a fluid approach that makes for fluent expression. Although it appears to be effervescent and elusive, it is nevertheless quite tangible. Ultimately, and often immediately, an improvisation can be captured, thought out, emotionally endowed— and all this will occur while one is in action on the keyboard, or other instrument, or with the voice.

It is legitimate to compare musical improvisations to the sketches or line drawings of a graphic artist. Do we look with condescension at the sketches of Rembrandt or the quick drawings of Picasso? We do not. Improvisation may fairly be compared to an artist's sketch, made with bold rhythmic strokes revealing direction, form, substance, and the quality of finished composition, but not including all details and final touches.

Today there is a steadily growing interest in the exciting art of improvisation here in the United States. One of the reasons that jazz is so appealing is the demonstrated ability of jazz musicians to improvise—and in groups. This interest has been spreading to the more classical musicians and laymen. Lukas Foss, for example, has been pioneering in ensemble improvising at the University of California at Los Angeles and demonstrating the results in various cities. Said Mr. Foss recently, "Ensemble improvisation is one of the oldest forms of making music. Even today, Oriental music is inconceivable without it, and so is Jazz. But in our serious Western music, ensemble improvisation has been obsolete for generations." Mr. Foss thereupon is setting about the invention of a technique that would make contemporary improvised chamber music possible.

Abroad, French organists have always recognized the value of improvisation for performance, and the Swiss (need one mention the name of Jaques-Dalcroze?) have for many years recognized the educational value of improvisation. And, of course the great musicians—Bach, Mozart, Beethoven, Chopin, Liszt—were masters of the art of extemporaneous composing. Indeed, is it not possible that the improvisations of Bach and Beethoven were sometimes even more inspired than their written compositions?

And the folk musicians? Where has our folk music stemmed from, if not from improvisation?

Africans today are known for their "controlled" improvisation, with complicated counterrhythms with drums. And the art of India, within its laws of music and dance, provides for subtle improvisations. Oriental music has always included improvisation and is today adding fresh facets to contemporary music; at the same time Oriental musicians are inquiring into American music, mainly in the field of the extempore.

For myself, improvisation is something like what is called "drinking from two streams." One stream is the flow of sounds within one, the subjective capacity to make music. The other is the objective musical heritage in the world around us. One dips into himself; one experiments with the larger vocabulary of musical language; one explores color, form, harmony, and contrapuntal studies.

The rewards of training in improvisation are many. First of all, there is keen satisfaction in learning to make decisions on the run; to find them good decisions is peculiarly exhilarating. But the reward of achieving an inner calm is even more satisfying. In order to improvise well, the mind must be collected and cool while one is working fast and emotions are at a high pitch. A strong feeling of rhythmic vitality is another valuable attribute. This vitality builds up confidence. One can create order out of what would otherwise be chaotic sound. It gives a feeling of mastery over material.

But the greatest reward is the feeling that one is functioning with more of his being than in ordinary circumstances. We are all familiar with the unsatisfactory feeling that we are employing only a part of our capabilities. Our minds may be doing most of the work, or we may be predominantly "emoting," or we may be engrossed in purely manual and instinctive living. Improvisation replaces this fractional living with wholeness. It makes a demand upon our minds, our emotions, and our motor capabilities at one and the same time. We must think, feel, and act simultaneously when we attempt to be extempore composers.

This explains why, when improvisation is going well, we have a sense of good, healthy functioning. Our whole being is awakened and called into action. What is more, the various parts of our psychology have to co-operate. There has to be teamwork of the directing mind, the excited emotions, and the nimble fingers. When these parts "click" with each other, we have a heightened sense of being. This teamwork, this harmony, is largely intuitive. We do not think things out, but see them in a flash.

In lifting for a time the quality and level of our lives, improvisation is an end in itself and its own reward.

Come, let us enter the rewarding world of improvisation.

CHAPTER II

When and How to Start Improvising

WHO IS eligible to start improvisation? I would answer that all those who are musically inclined and eager, whether they have had any previous training, are candidates for this lively art. Anybody, let me repeat, who really wishes to make music and is curious about the processes of music-making is eligible to begin here and now.

The approach offered in this book and the accompanying exercises have been successfully used by students of all ages, including children. It is hoped that this approach will also inspire "self-starters." Even for those ten-minutes-a-day people who love to play and want to play and even go on musical explorations, self-instruction in improvisation can be cumulative and give rewarding results.

The aim is to help the student to free himself—to help him to find his own motivation and tap its deepest sources. There is a healthy, growing tendency among music teachers today to encourage students to explore in the vast field of music rather than to learn to play a few pieces for recitals. Teachers today reject merely surface performance as a goal for their pupils, and try instead to help the pupil reach deeper levels within himself and to make more inspired music from within.

Improvisation is a direct approach to music-making. It avoids the usual frustrations attendant upon early music lessons. Improvisation is, in fact, an exciting introduction to all music-making.

We shall appeal to primal impulses, for improvisation springs from a primal stirring by means of drum or voice before the piano and other complex instruments were evolved.

In teaching music it has been found that certain barriers are removed when people become warmed up. Through rhythmic exercises and music drills, their feelings are stirred. A feeling of frustration is driven away and a buoyant state enters. There are playfulness and humor, but not at the expense of control. The thinking process goes on and a sense of wholeness prevails.

To state it another way, the aim of this book is to present specific techniques without pedagogical clutter, and to use analogy and example in such a positive way that the concept, the flow, and even the correct physical (muscular) memory may be captured and developed during the student's workouts by himself.

The principles of improvisation are the same, no matter what the instrument—xylophone or recorder, voice, piano, or other instrument. Certain exercises will be slanted toward the piano, but adaptation of them to other instruments can be made easily.

How then do we start improvisation? We start by acquiring a vocabulary of musical elements. The elements that appear in a complete improvisation are rhythm, melody, harmony, form, counterpoint, and imagination. These elements combine to form a unity that expresses the improviser's concept and produces fluent music-making. This unity is brought about by the directing mind, the excited emotions, and the agile fingers, while the elements named above blend in the playing.

But the first stage in the study of improvisation is the experiencing of each of these elements. Then we shall practice blending them until all function simultaneously and form an organic whole.

Thus we begin by gaining a vocabulary of rhythms and a vocabulary of melody-making, a vocabulary of harmony and counterpoint, a vocabulary even of form; we shall blend all of these with imagination and we shall then find that a certain vitality has been generated and that vitality confers on us the freedom to compose music spontaneously.

CHAPTER III

Rhythm—the Initiating Force

RHYTHM is the energizing force that generates action. Rhythm is derived from a Greek word that means measured motions. It is movement in time. Stated more exactly, rhythm is, in the words of Frederick Schlieder, "the governing principle in the ordering of movement of tones in the element of time."

It is usual to say that rhythm was present in the universe before man came into being. Rhythm is in the movement of the planets and in the recurrence of the seasons. Rhythm is in nature—in the duality of day and night, in the twofold action of ocean tides. Rhythm is the basis of such vital human functions as breathing and the beating of the heart.

The metric relationships of rhythm are based on a fundamental succession of regular pulsations. Rhythm includes the *beat* and its *rebound.* A group of beats forms a measure, then measures form phrases, and the rhythmic movement of phrases becomes longer in form. Rhythm, as we shall see, can stand alone without melody, even without musical tone.

To gain a practical sense of rhythm, consider the rhythm of ocean waves. In certain prints of Hokusai, we may get a marvelous feeling of visual rhythm as we look at his great waves. We may stand on the seashore and watch the waves move *out* from the shore and in —*out* and in, and *out* and in, in relation to the shore. Then, instead of merely watching the waves, try responding to this rhythm; move with it; feel it. Feel the inevitable return of the wave from the shore. Anticipate the forward-and-back movements of the waves.

Now, if you can, experiment with a child in a swing. Give the swing a good shove forward. The better the start you give him, the more often the child will swing back and forth. This demonstrates the prime nature of rhythm. The swing is like a pendulum set in motion, for it swings back by itself. You don't have to pull it back. The impulse starts it and the movement continues by itself. You can trust the swing-back, or the rebound.

Trusting the rebound is the beginning of improvisation.

EXERCISE 1 — $\frac{2}{4}$ Meter

Let us start with a very simple exercise in $\frac{2}{4}$ meter. The 4, here, stands for quarter notes, which in this exercise you can think of as "walking" notes, as representing a steady, walking pace. The 2 above the 4 in $\frac{2}{4}$ meter indicates that there are two quarter notes (walking notes) or their equivalent in duration in every measure.

Now walk—beat a drum—tap on a table—or clap, to get this $\frac{2}{4}$ rhythm. Start the first beat with a good impulse. Expect the rebound. Let the second beat rebound out of the first. Keep this going. Notice that the first beat is stronger, the second beat lighter.

Now clap the rhythm, counting aloud, | 1 2 | 1 2 | 1 2 | 1 2 ||. Imitate a ball bouncing. Bounce on 1, let it rebound on 2.

The bar-line comes before count 1, the strong beat. Don't let the bar-line stop you. It does not represent a fence, but exists simply to indicate that the strong beat is coming next. Moving or clapping in time to the rhythm helps you to establish the pulse clearly.

EXERCISE 2 — $\frac{3}{4}$ Meter

In $\frac{3}{4}$ meter there are three beats in each measure—three quarter notes or their equivalent in duration. A waltz is in $\frac{3}{4}$ meter. So is a minuet.

Clap it, gathering enough energy on the first beat to carry you through the two other beats.

EXERCISE 3 — $\frac{4}{4}$ Meter

In $\frac{4}{4}$ meter you have 4 beats to each measure.

The second, third, and fourth beats spring out of the first beat. Marches are usually in $\frac{4}{4}$ meter.

March and count in $\frac{4}{4}$ meter, or if you prefer, try "marching" with the index and third fingers on the piano ledge, or table, with steady, lively pulse.

EXERCISE 4 — $\frac{6}{8}$ Meter

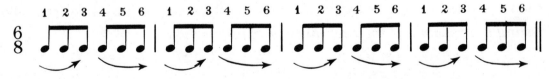

This is a compound rhythm, *two*-swing, forward and return, with three beats in each swing. Swing your arm, counting 1 2 3 to the forward swing and 4 5 6 within the return swing.

For a clearer conception of $\frac{6}{8}$ meter in motion, picture a gondola on the water. The gondolier stands and poles a long stroke with his oar on every first beat. That propels the boat forward for the whole measure. At the same time, imagine the water sways the gondola to one side on the first three beats, and slightly to the other side on the last three beats. Feel the swing of it. Sway with it as you count the time. This process must not be merely theoretical. You must experience the motion, preferably with some outward movement. The freer you feel to exaggerate the motion at first, the better.

One may accurately speak of the orchestral conductor as the leader who sets the music going and allows for the rebound. If he is a capable conductor, he will not push his orchestra on to produce every note and beat. Instead he *lets* it happen and moves on the wave of the music. At the same time, he has a very broad conception of the whole composition.

Observe a good conductor. Watch his wide sweeping movements when the interpretation requires them. Note, in contrast, how little outward motion the conductor makes when passages speak for themselves and the men in the orchestra understand and need scarcely a sign to indicate what the composer is saying.

Cast yourself as the conductor of an imaginary orchestra or chorus. Require of yourself that you feel the pulse of the music so strongly that you are able to project and express with conviction the rhythm you are feeling within. To meet this requirement, one must sometimes break through old patterns and old associations, and undertake to work with music material in a very exaggerated way.

EXERCISE 5 — Conducting

For conducting the basic rhythms, hold a pencil or stick in your right hand like a baton. You will discover that you give a little up-beat before moving downward, for count 1.

When you improvise, or conduct, or play an instrument, the up-beat is a vital part of the rhythmic experience. It anticipates the down-beat.

In $\frac{2}{4}$ meter, the up-beat is count 2.
This is the way the up-beat looks in $\frac{2}{4}$ meter. Try to feel this.

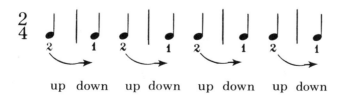

You probably have noticed that when you wish to keep a swing moving back and forth for some time, you pull the swing far back and as high as you can before you start it going. That pull-back is like a preliminary up-beat. The baseball pitcher "winds up" before throwing the ball. You see an up-beat movement in the diver as he rebounds from the springboard before curving downward into the water. You can experience this up-beat movement with the dancer even before you witness his high leap from the wings onto the stage. Sometimes you hear the rush of it in a rapidly ascending passage in a full orchestra. The conductor, his arms moving forcefully upward, anticipates the up-beat before the descent to the down-beat, and then the music moves of its own volition. It is the impetus in the up-beat which gives power and flow to the following down-beat, and this sets the work in motion.

The motion need not always be vigorous. Sometimes there is a gentle up-beat, as in a courtly minuet; there is a gentle rise as the partners step forward, and likewise just before they face each other in a stately bow.

An up-beat phrase naturally starts on any beat except the first. The up-beat acts to lift one over the bar-line to the down-beat without a halt.

Specific dance patterns like the minuet, bourrée, and gavotte often start on up-beats, as follows:

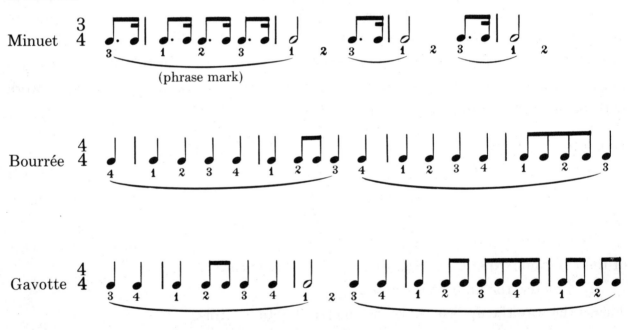

Notice that if a phrase starts on the third count, it ends on the second count (in $\frac{3}{4}$ meter).

Phrases starting on 3 end on 2 (in $\frac{4}{4}$ meter).

If you feel the pattern throughout the piece, the music will never sound heavy. In playing, the muscles and fingers will respond with elasticity and buoyancy.

The question may arise of why we dwell on the technique of the conductor's beat. What does it have to do with improvisation?

You have to be your own conductor when improvising.

EXERCISE 6 — Conducting

Say and conduct:

$\frac{2}{4}$	down	up		down	up	
	1	2		1	2	

$\frac{3}{4}$	down	out	up	down	out	up	
	1	2	3	1	2	3	

$\frac{4}{4}$	down	in	out	up	down	in	out	up	
	1	2	3	4	1	2	3	4	

NOTE: *Out* indicates away from the body. *In* means toward the body.

Play a favorite record and be its conductor. Feel the dynamics and the flow. Lead spontaneously, projecting forcefully your concept of the composer's music idea.

When improvising you must be prepared to project an invigorated rhythmic state similar to that you feel as a conductor.

In doing the previous exercises, you have felt the flow of several measures in succession. This is the beginning of phrase feeling, similar to speaking a simple sentence or a question.

A single measure no more exists by itself in music than a single word exists by itself in language. From the beginning, music has built upon the phrase. Gradually a whole rhythmic structure has been built, often dependent upon the energy which the rhythmic impulse generated at the start.

Sometimes an extended form grows out of the continuation, the extension, of a musical idea, somewhat as a theme ramifies in a conversation. A kind of "free association" comes into play. The end of a phrase or a special rhythmic design may excite the imagination and invite you to continue with it, but care must be taken to avoid wandering. You will need to return to the theme or near the original rhythm at intervals. Stick to the subject, but do not be stuck with it.

But before continuing with the development of phrases and longer time spans, it is desirable at this point to say something about rhythmic patterns.

Obviously music would become dull if we used only steady quarter notes all the time. One does not always walk. Sometimes one runs, or skips, or gallops, or hops, or dances, or pauses: one's choice depends on mood and purpose. There are many movements to express emotions and ideas. Let us relate these movements to rhythm patterns in music. We shall find that sometimes very fast notes and syncopations (shifting of regular accent) and rests (silences) in unexpected places present themselves as we become aware of the possibilities.

What possibilities are there in basic meters? Exploring for patterns is vital in improvisation. It is one of the mental activities through which one develops the tools to build a music vocabulary. It is a way of thinking for improvisation, and eventually it is a means of being at home in it.

There are two aspects to this exploration: 1) the search for the basic patterns which allow for variation; 2) the discovery that the basic patterns are not endless. Combinations of basic patterns are endless, however, and in the exploration of these we find great variety as well as delight.

In $\frac{2}{4}$ meter certain basic patterns will be within the frame of the following:

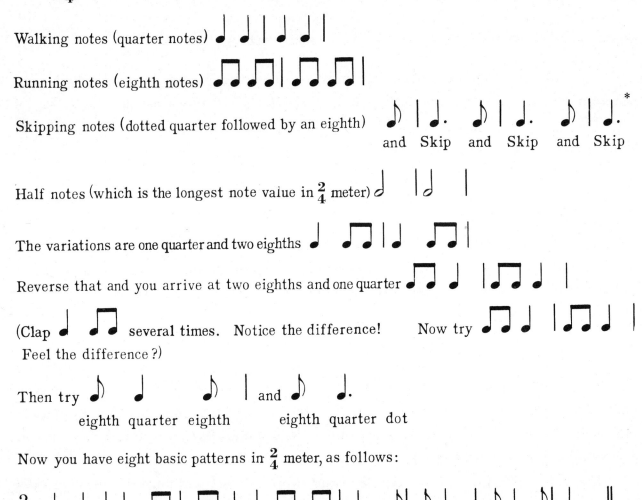

Walking notes (quarter notes)

Running notes (eighth notes)

Skipping notes (dotted quarter followed by an eighth)

and Skip and Skip and Skip

Half notes (which is the longest note value in $\frac{2}{4}$ meter)

The variations are one quarter and two eighths

Reverse that and you arrive at two eighths and one quarter

(Clap   several times. Notice the difference!   Now try
Feel the difference ?)

Then try
eighth quarter eighth   eighth quarter dot

Now you have eight basic patterns in $\frac{2}{4}$ meter, as follows:

(1)   (2)   (3)   (4)   (5)   (6)   (7)   (8)

* Students are uncertain about the value of a dot after a note. The rule is: a dot after a note adds half of the value of the note preceding it. Therefore, the quarter note with dot after it ♩. gets 1½ counts (equal to a quarter note and an eighth note), followed by another eighth note to complete the beat.

Say, "Quarter—dot—eighth" and clap it.

In the dotted-note measures, be sure to hold the dotted note (the long note) long enough and let the short one move quickly and lightly on to the next beat. *The dotted quarter note followed by an eighth is very useful.*

Clap the above rhythms often. Through repetition gain the difference in feeling between them. This activity is like that of a painter who tries not only different colors but also different shades of the same color, or draws a series of short lines as opposed to longer, "slower" lines. When you understand these differences in feeling, you can use these rhythm patterns in your music-making as part of your own vocabulary—to convey more action, vitality, or contrast.

Now choose any two of the eight basic patterns given below, and keep clapping them until you feel free with them. Gradually try other combinations. For discovering the rhythm patterns in $\frac{3}{4}$ $\frac{4}{4}$ and $\frac{6}{8}$ meters, it is a good practice to work them out for yourself.

Here is a clue: Take the $\frac{2}{4}$ patterns and add a quarter note (or two eighth notes) to each measure, thus making $\frac{3}{4}$ meter. To this add another quarter note (or two eighth notes) for $\frac{4}{4}$ meter.

In $\frac{3}{4}$ meter, using this way of thinking, you will find at least twenty-five different patterns. You will find well over fifty different patterns in $\frac{4}{4}$ meter.

For more exciting rhythms try these:

The simplest phrase in music is often a four-measure phrase. It is somewhat like a very simple sentence, such as a child might say: "The cat drinks milk." This is an analogy only, for in music we do not think in words. We express music-making through rhythm, sound, dynamics.

In $\frac{2}{4}$ meter, the first phrase might be ♩ ♩ |♩ ♩ |♩ ♩ |♩ |

Clap it and feel the whole of it.

When you bounce a ball, it springs back by itself. This time, start your *phrase* with enough impulse to carry you through the whole phrase without a break. After you feel the phrase length in $\frac{2}{4}$ meter, then try the flow of four-measure phrases in $\frac{3}{4}, \frac{4}{4}$, and $\frac{6}{8}$ meters.

You will soon wish to produce a longer form than a four-measure phrase. The motive-and-complement—often called question-and-answer—is a good next step. Here is an approach I have found useful with a child and equally useful for an adult. To introduce question-and-answer, I say to the child:

"When we have conversations, and someone asks a question, where is the voice at the end of the question?"

The child generally answers, "Up."

"And when you answer the question, where does your voice land?"

"Oh, it lands down," says the child.

"Now I'll ask you a question in rhythm sounds, and you answer it in rhythm sounds. You understand, of course, that we do not have any real words in mind."

Now, so that the rhythm may remain unbroken, it is important to respond immediately. Because, in music, one is filling a time-space with rhythmic patterns, sound, and dynamics, the pulsation cannot be stopped and broken into by hesitation. We want no holes in the time-space.

I clap a music phrase, leaving it suspended in anticipation of an answer. Sometimes the pupil just waits—nothing happens. If he does not respond, or if uncertainty appears, I "ask a question" on the drum, so that he can answer that rhythm on the drum. If he still hesitates, I sometimes say, "Music-making is something like diving. Before you dive, you stand on the springboard and watch the water and wish that you could dive in, but nothing happens. Then suddenly you do decide to plunge, and there you go! Try the same idea on the drum. I'll start and clap a question, and you just dive in and answer." Then we continue and usually these spontaneous rhythms are very good. This response is important, psychologically, for the student. If he can get beyond the first "I can't" and accomplish a response which supplies an "I can," he is proceeding in a positive direction.

Soon he is ready to be the leader and to ask the question himself. I supply the answer. In the balancing phrase, I sometimes repeat part of the design of his question. But to a beginner I say nothing about the technique of using part of his motif in the complement, because, fundamentally, the rhythm must speak directly. He will sense these phases and use them when he is ready to take them on. The less said in words, the better. Soon the student is ready to improvise both his own question and the answer—the motive-and-complement.

The next step for him is an expansion of the question-and-answer into a longer form which can be compared to a conversation. He picks up the thread of the first question-and-answer, then goes on, extending the phrases at various points—possibly interrupting the line with an exclamation or an assent, then introducing a new idea (contrast in music), and finally comes to the conclusion.

Again I must stress that we do not use words as props. When a student produces a poem of his own which may have grown out of the rhythmic drills, and he wishes to set it to his own music, or sets a poem or a psalm to his own music, then we include meaningful words.

ACCENT. There are three kinds of accents in music: the metric, the phrasal, and the emotional.

1. Metric: The accent comes on the down-beat, the first beat of each measure (the first beat after the bar-line).

2. Phrasal: The beginning of each phrase has a qualitatively different accent, often related to up-beat. It is like watching someone enter a room. The very fact that he enters gives an impression of accent. A kind of recognition takes place. In the same way, when a new musical phrase enters, you recognize its beginning by a slight accent. This is different from, and subtler than, the metric accent. The metric must continue to be the underlying pulse, and at the same time the phrase accent has its role.

3. Emotional: The height (or depth) of a phrase or a series of phrases; at the height of the climax there is a special accent. The composer may lead up to it by a crescendo (gradually louder) or a diminuendo (gradually softer), or by a sequence of phrases. Suddenly you arrive at the top, the pinnacle. There is an accent to mark this. This need not always be loud. Beethoven often surprises with a pianissimo (very soft—*pp*) where you would expect a loud climax. That *pp* accent can be tremendously impressive and exciting—like a whisper when you're expecting a shout.

Watch for these three kinds of accent. Recognize the function of each. All three move within each music composition. Experiment with these three types of accent until you grasp for yourself their expression and proportion within one piece. By working with them now, you will be prepared to include them in the melody-making described in the next chapter.

EXERCISE 8 — Rhythm Techniques

Begin to experiment with the following, less familiar rhythm techniques. You will find them stimulating to work with.

The following rhythms—$\frac{6}{8}$ $\frac{9}{8}$ and $\frac{12}{8}$—are compounds of $\frac{2}{4}$ $\frac{3}{4}$ and $\frac{6}{8}$.

Count aloud and conduct:

swing   swing
forward   back

Sing, for example, the "Skye Boat Song" or other tune in $\frac{6}{8}$ meter and swing your arm with this rhythm. This is a compound 2 time, where in each measure there is the feeling of two movements, a swing forward with the first three beats and a swing back with the other three beats.

Count aloud and conduct:

swing   swing   swing
down   right   up

This is a compound 3 meter, where there are three large movements in each measure, and three beats within each movement.

See the $\frac{9}{8}$ pattern in the Béla Bartók *Mikrokosmos,* Book V, No. 132.

Count aloud and conduct:

swing   swing   swing   swing
down   left   right   up

This is a compound 4 time, where there are four large movements in each measure, and three beats within each of the four movements.

Note the rhythmic pattern of the Gigue from the A-Minor Partita of Bach, below.

Aaron Copland on polyrhythms is instructive.

"Our polyrhythms are [more] characteristically the deliberate setting one against the other, of a steady pulse with a free pulse. Its most familiar manifestation is in the small jazz band combination, where the so-called rhythm section provides the grand metrics around which the melody instruments can freely invent rhythms of their own. . . . The typical feature of our rhythm was this juxtaposition of steadiness, either implied or actually heard, as against freedom of rhythmic invention . . . ex. 'swinging a tune' . . . simply means that over a steady ground rhythm the singer or instrumentalist toys with the beat, never exactly on it, but either anticipating it or lagging behind it in gradations of metrical units so subtle that our notational system has no way of indicating it. Of course you cannot stay off the beat unless you know where that beat is. Here freedom is interesting only in relation to regularity . . . on the other hand when our better jazz bands wish to be rhythmically exact they come down on the beat with trip-hammer precision."

EXERCISE 9 — Rhythm Techniques

Here are basic rhythms in $\frac{5}{4}$ meter.

Do not try to feel each measure as an extended four-beat measure, and do not hold the last beat, which would make the measure feel as if it had six beats. Count five beats in each measure. (See Béla Bartók "Bulgarian Rhythm," No. 115, Book IV, *Mikrokosmos,* and Bartók No. 120, Book IV, *Mikrokosmos.*)

Expression through changing meters (as in the example below) may be influenced by the fact that when people are excited their pulse is likely to change; it not only gets faster, but also sometimes becomes uneven. This can be exciting in improvisation. Uneven meter can prove stirring in the rhythms of modern music, as well as in folk song and dance.

EXERCISE 10 — Uneven Meter and Uneven Phrase Lengths

Musical phrases do not need to balance each other symmetrically. Note how the eight measures of each example below are divided. Experiment with uneven phrases. Group the following eight measures in ways other than a question-and-answer:

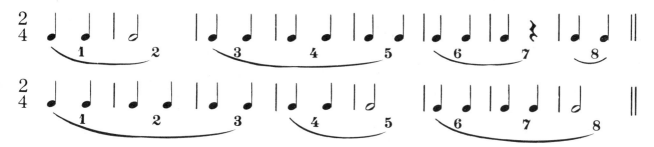

Find other ways of grouping measures into uneven phrase lengths; clap them until they become part of your vocabulary. Example: Subdivide ten measures:

Block out the measures as follows and try many different rhythmic patterns. Example:

1 | 2 | 3 | 4 | 5 | 6 | 7 | 8 | 9 | 10 ‖

EXERCISE 11 — Rhythmic Counterpoint (Movement of at Least Two Rhythmic Lines)

Tap this out on your lap or on a table top—one pattern with your left hand, the other pattern at the same time with your right hand. Then invert, i.e., let the left-hand (L.H.) pattern become the right-hand (R.H.) pattern, and so on. Realize two individual lines moving at once.

Next, try alternate movement with a tie, which is a curved line joining two identical notes and indicating that the second note is not sounded, but is held. You may feel that second note as a "suppressed accent." Notice that when one part has more movement, the other part is sustained, held over by a tie.

Start on the second beat—an up-beat.

NOTE: The musical symbol ♩ is a rest (silence) equal to a quarter note; the musical symbol ━ is a rest (silence) equal to a whole note.

Include syncopation.

Henry Cowell, in *New Musical Resources,* has defined cross-rhythm (counterrhythm) as "two or more parts playing different systems of rhythms against each other."

Here is a basic type of two systems playing against each other. One system is in 3 time, and the other is in 4 time.

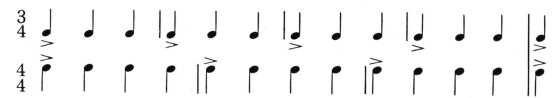

Notice that after twelve beats (*i.e.,* on every thirteenth beat) they arrive together.

EXERCISE 12 — Cross-rhythms

First, let one person clap one part and a second person take the other. Reverse this. Then let one person try both parts, tapping one rhythm with the right hand, the other with the left. This sounds particularly good with various rhythmic patterns on drums and when using unusual scales.

The following is a four-drum rhythm of a bamba dance out of Africa:

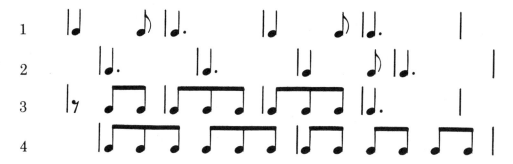

EXERCISE 13 — Syncopated Rhythms

Devise syncopated rhythms, feeling 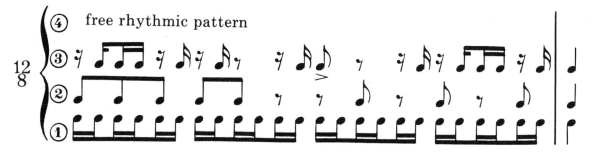 (sixteenths) as minute metrical units.

This is for group improvisation. Start with No. 1, the basic rhythm, add No. 2. Next time around add No. 3, and finally include the free rhythmic patterns while 1, 2, and 3 are continuing.

As you work on these basic patterns, you will gradually include the more or less involved rhythms that may be part of your own individual make-up. This enlarged vocabulary grows partly out of your collective past, out of the stream of your own native heritage. Folk-rhythms, jazz idioms, chants, or complicated counterrhythms may rise to the surface.

Be ready to reach the quiet center within yourself where the source of inspiration exists. When improvising, we must reach that level where both the native heritage and your developing musicianship exist.

As you apply the procedures given so far, you will soon find your own natural rhythmic expression. Do not force the growth or search for odd or extreme forms of expression. Your music will evolve naturally, gradually, and wholeheartedly, while realizing that rhythm is the primal, energizing force that generates action.

CHAPTER IV

Melody-Making

W E SHALL begin the melody work by singing one tone that should be chosen within the range of your voice. Establish that tone, which we shall call the "home tone" (also called key tone). Start from that sound and, while clapping or conducting the rhythm, let other tones move out from the "home tone," and after a little motion in sound, return to the "home tone." In this way we shall begin to establish a sense of tonal relationship, with a place to start from and return to, within our own feelings, while forming a simple design in sound, with rhythm.

In this exercise sing a scale; for example, beginning with C. We then have in our scale C D E F G A B C—the eight notes of the octave. The intervals between the tones are whole steps except the intervals between E and F, B and C, which are half-steps.

In the diagram below, we indicate a scale of two octaves and a pitch picture. We move scalewise, which means that we progress from tone to adjacent tone without skipping any intervals, and start and finish on the home tone.

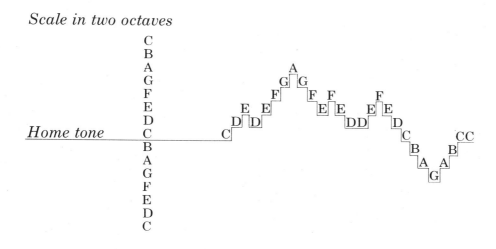

From your vocabulary of rhythmic patterns choose one and apply it to your scale tune. Then choose two patterns. Clap them and then apply to your scalewise designs. Gradually apply all rhythmic patterns in $\frac{2}{4}$ $\frac{3}{4}$ $\frac{4}{4}$ and $\frac{6}{8}$ meters.

EXERCISE 14 — Pitch Pictures

Try pitch pictures while improvising tunes. Let the pitch rise or fall as your melody line rises and falls. Keep it simple.

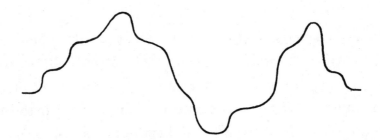

Try this with more motion—some quarter notes and some eighth notes.

This time it was not finished, was it?

Now let's start it again and finish it.

This is the beginning of question-and-answer:

The voice at the end of the question is up.

When you answer the question, your voice lands down.

You will notice that in the first example above, where there was a suspended melody, an answer was required. One was given in the second example.

Sing a question in music sounds and answer it in music sounds.

Sing a music phrase, leaving the melody suspended, anticipating an answer. Balance the question by supplying the answer. In order to keep the rhythm unbroken, it is important to respond immediately. Because, in music, one is filling up a time-space with patterns and sound, the pulsation cannot be stopped and broken by hesitation. Again, we want no holes in the time-space. We must keep going. Let the rhythm generate the impulse to keep the tune moving.

Fundamentally the rhythm must speak directly.

After you have sung many questions-and-answers, you may wish to try them on an instrument.

Of course the instrument need not be the piano. Use a good xylophone or recorder (wooden flute), other wind or string instruments, or piano; the principle applies to all instruments. But the voice often brings out the most intimate expression of melody. As soon as one approaches an instrument, that instrument itself tempts one to use it as a palette for experimenting with sound. You are likely to improvise melodies that are not so much a part of yourself as they are when you express your music feeling and ideas with your own voice. However, using the instrument as a palette brings forward many new and different possibilities for experimenting with sound and rhythm.

EXERCISE 15 — The Beginning of Melody-Making

At this point, however, let us use the piano. Start on middle C with your index finger, while feeling the basic rhythm (keep to $\frac{2}{4}$ time at first); using only the index finger, move up-a-way (to the right), down-a-way (to the left), forming a little design while moving away from C, approximately scalewise, and with not too many skips at first, and when ready, returning to C. That's what we call "scale tune," and it is the beginning of melody-making on an instrument.

You may wonder why we suggest moving scalewise. The explanation is that if there are too many skips, the tunes are apt to sound somewhat like broken chords, for example C—E—G—C—E. The broken-chord type of tune often becomes dull, unless balanced by scalewise line to form flowing melody.

Next try wider skips. Then use some stepwise motion and some skips. You will soon find certain favorite progressions. Listen carefully and decide which successions sound best to you. In Chapter V, where we explain the use of unusual scales, you will find that it is best to move approximately scalewise in order to maintain the full value and the best expression of each specific scale.

After improvising question-and-answer, you will find it refreshing to break the phrases in different ways and also to produce longer phrases.

Imagine a group of people in conversation. One introduces a subject. Another makes a brief comment. Another amplifies—extends the idea. Somebody interrupts with a question. Then somebody picks up the thread and continues it. An exclamation may interrupt, but finally the thought is brought to a conclusion.

EXERCISE 16 — "Conversation"

Try to carry this idea of a conversation over into your music-making, but not with the thought of words. Do not be overly concerned about the form or about when to stop. Keep moving rhythmically. Make the "conversation" as long as you can, as this will stretch your power to make melody. Gradually your melodies will become more consistent and more unified. Here we are not so interested in consistency or in producing balanced phrases as in expanding melodically. Note that this exercise is just the opposite of the more usual and obviously balanced question-and-answer—motive-and-complement.

Next try melody with interruptions. (See the Bartók *Mikrokosmos,* Book III, No. 83.)

EXERCISE 17 — Echo

A playful yet disciplined approach is the echo.

Sing a short phrase, loudly (*ff*).

Echo it precisely, very softly (*pp*).

If you find this easier to start with words, you may sing something like "hello" or "loo la lay" for the vowel sounds. In Chapter VII, "How to Listen," I have included a song called "By'm Bye" (a folk song arranged by Ruth Crawford Seeger in *American Folk Songs for Children*), which makes a good echo game. Mozart's *"Cache-cache,"* in the ballet *Les Petits riens,* is an exhilarating piece that also lends itself to the echo (see Page 166, "Rhythm Drawings and Pitch Pictures").

The echo can become the beginning of disciplined work, for you are invited to repeat the exact phrase. Too, the contrast of loud and soft will be useful toward building longer forms later.

After singing the exact echo, try to vary it. Sing a phrase loudly, echo it softly, then try it higher, lower, inverted, in different rhythmic patterns, etc. Play with it.

Another way to continue a melodic improvisation is to become aware of how a phrase ends. Often the last few measures are the most interesting. Is this because one becomes more relaxed toward the end of a long phrase, thus favoring an interesting turn in the music? This last turn will initiate a fresh though related idea that can sometimes become the germ of a whole new section. It often arrives at the "psychological moment" so that these last few measures of the musical sentence can be used to good effect as the beginning of another sentence. This germ or kernel sounds very different as the beginning of a fresh sentence (or section) from the way it sounded as the end of the first sentence.

Too, the fresh beginning often acts as a springboard toward developing a new, yet consistent, follow-up.

EXERCISE 18 — Motive-and-Complement

To move on to the next, more formal arrangement, here are the steps for producing motive, motive repeated, balanced by the complement:

Sing a two-measure motive, repeat it, and balance it by a four-measure complement.

1. Clap it.
2. Sing it while clapping.
3. Play it.
4. Use various rhythmic patterns within this frame while clapping, singing, then playing.
5. Reverse the pattern by having the long four-measure phrase first, balanced by two short phrases.
6. Improvise, using this phrase pattern.

Do not limit this to a two-measure motive. It can be shorter or somewhat longer. Experiment with a three-measure motive and see where that leads you. You may find the balancing phrases to be somewhat like this, rhythmically:

Continue, using similar rhythmic patterns.

EXERCISE 19 — Rotation, Repeated Note, Opposite Motion

It is important to learn the technique for improvising wide leaps in the melodic line, for singing and playing. This provides contrast to scalewise motion and adds vigor to the music.

ROTATION

Rotate around a note (C in the example below) before the wide leap up or down, then move in opposite direction.

REPEATED NOTE

Gather enough energy while reiterating one repeated note to make you wish to take a wide skip in the melodic line.

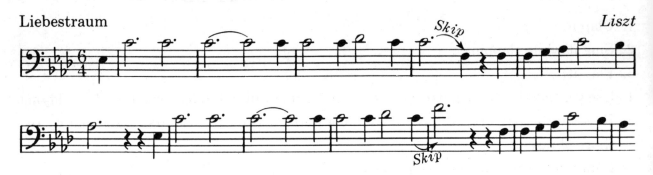

OPPOSITE MOTION

Here, before you take the big skip, you move in the direction opposite to it. This motion can be compared to the ball player where he swings his arm backward just before he throws the ball.

Direction: Swing your arm as if you were about to throw a ball and then throw it. Next trace this line with your finger on the staff. Now play.

Besides being used for preparation for a wide skip in the melody line, these three devices are useful in themselves. Rotation can be used as pure decoration. A mordent is a rotation surrounding one tone, and was originally used for decoration (somewhat in the way a grace note 𝄐 is used) and also for accent (especially when the keyboard instruments were not so powerful and resonant as today's piano). Repeated notes are also useful for accent. Include experiments with opposite motion, for added interest in melodic line. You will soon find the values in this approach for yourself.

EXERCISE 20 — Up-beat

Do not start the up-beat on the key tone (C in the example below), but let the up-beat be an anticipation of it. The strong down-beat will probably land on the key tone for the first measure.

For experiments in range, try a question in high range on the piano and put your answer in low range. Imagine the tone color of the flute for the question and the low tones of the cello for the answering phrase. Then think of the violin as contrasted with the bassoon, soprano with bass, viola with clarinet. This almost implies that the soprano area (the question) will continue after the lower voice enters. This also suggests the beginning of two-part counterpoint.

As previously observed, there are three kinds of accents.

1. Metric: A strong beat (pulse) accent at the beginning—down-beat—of every measure.
2. Phrasal: At beginning of each phrase, there is a different kind of accent, often related to up-beat. Start on a note other than the key tone.
3. Emotional: The feeling for the rise or fall of the line (the melodic line), stressing the peak.

Work on each of these accents separately, and gradually you will feel the co-ordination of the three, for in a good improvisation all three are expressed within the same frame.

SEQUENCE

A "sequence" is a short series of tones, or a figure repeated, each time a note higher or a note lower, or at different levels in the scale.

In the Bach C-Major Invention the sequence is repeated each time two notes lower.

Here are the same measures, but in the bass.

Later you will see the value of sequence for modulation.

EXERCISE 21 — Beginning of Transposition

By now you should be ready to transpose tunes to many keys.

Number the scale of C: C D E F G A B C
                        1 2 3 4 5 6 7 8

Pick out the following tunes on your instrument, then transpose them to other keys, applying the number system in each new key.

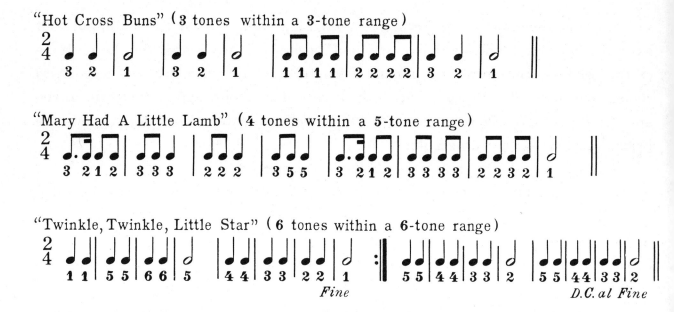

"Hot Cross Buns" (3 tones within a 3-tone range)

"Mary Had A Little Lamb" (4 tones within a 5-tone range)

"Twinkle, Twinkle, Little Star" (6 tones within a 6-tone range)

At first, reproduce the same progressions as the C-major scale in a different key by raising or lowering the pitch.

It is possible to pick out all scales—at first with one finger; for example: Play and sing C♯. Now sing the C♯ scale, one tone at a time, starting on C♯ and matching each sound of your sung note to the one on the piano. Do it slowly, listening carefully. You will soon feel as free with the "black keys" on the piano as you do with the white ones. Soon you can continue with all scales and improvise tunes in the same way. This is not difficult.

Next, write out each scale. Then play it with one finger. Combine looking at your written scale and feeling for the scale with one finger (index finger) on the keyboard. For correct fingering, first find the places in the scale where the thumb would naturally come— on the white notes (it would be awkward on the black notes)!

Transposing your melodies will gradually become easy as you learn to trust your ear and acquire the additional knowledge of the simple mechanics of scale structure.

There is a way of thinking about scales so that you can see them as *one* concept. This is known as the "Circle of Keys." *All* the major scales are only transpositions of the key of C. Note that in all major scales the half-steps and the whole steps are in the same relative positions. The same relative sounds are expressed on different levels of the same structure.

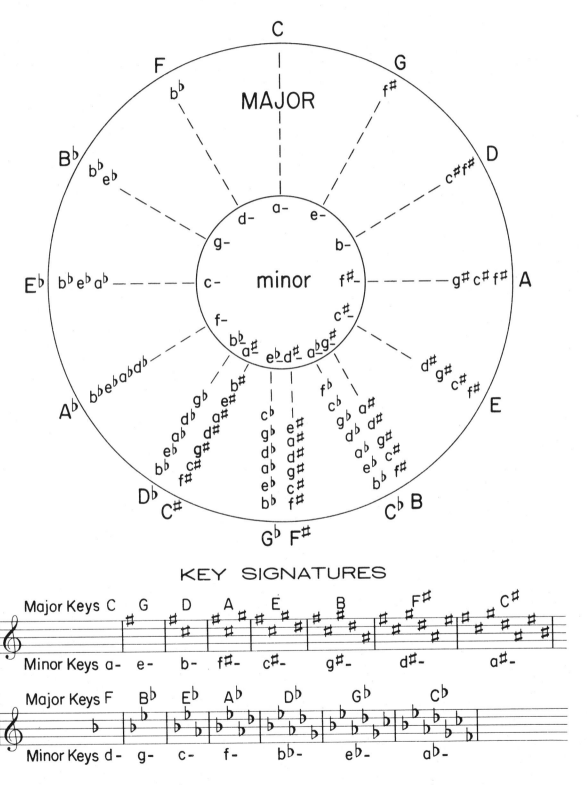

KEY SIGNATURES

Become familiar with the whole circle of keys. (Writing it out is a good device.) The scales with sharps line up on the right side of the circle, the scales with flats on the left side. For scales with more sharps or flats, the new ones are added to those already in line.

You seldom have to play pieces with more than four or five sharps or flats, but it is a good idea to get the principle of all the major and minor scales at the same time. To begin, take the C-major scale. Before playing the notes, place your fingers in the left hand over C D E F with the fourth, third, second, and first fingers. Then with the right hand place the thumb on G, second finger on A, third on B, fourth on C.

4 3 2 1   1 2 3 4

C D E F   G A B C

L.H.   R.H.

Next play C D E F with the left hand and G A B C with the right. Now place the left hand over the notes you are holding in the right hand. Move the right hand up to the next group of four notes and then play G A B C D E F♯ G, which is the G-major scale. Note that what was formerly the *upper* group of four notes now becomes the *lower* group of four notes. (Each of these groups is called a tetrachord.)

4 3 2 1   1 2 3 4

G A B C   D E F♯ G

L.H.   R.H.

Now continue to replace the four tones that you have in the right hand with the left hand and add the upper four notes.

4 3 2 1   1 2 3 4

D E F♯ G   A B C♯ D

L.H.   R.H.

What key do you now have? The key of D major. What sharps does the key of D have? Answer: two sharps. F♯ and C♯. Notice that the last sharp, C♯ in this case, is one-half step below the key tone, D in this case.

Now continue through the circle of major keys. When you arrive at the scale of C♯ major you will have completed the seven sharp keys. Keeping your fingers over the notes in the scale of C♯, call C♯ D♭. This is known as an "enharmonic change," and the sound of the scale of D♭ major is the same as the sound of C♯-major scale on the piano. (On the violin it would be slightly different.) Now recite the scale of D♭ major as you play it. A short cut in remembering the order of the flats is that the first four flats spell B E A D.

Too, the next to the last flat is the key tone. For example, in the key of D♭ we have five flats, B E A D G. The next to the last flat is D♭, therefore the key tone is D♭. Play the D♭-major scale again.

You will notice on the chart that G♭ major and F♯ major are also enharmonic, and the scales of C♭ major and B major are enharmonic.

Continue the circle of keys through the flat keys as you did with the sharps.

For practice, write out the key signatures of all the major scales.

RELATIVE MINOR KEYS

Each major scale has its relative *minor* scale, which is found 1½ steps (the distance of a minor third) below the key tone of its major scale. The relative minor scale has the same key signature as its relative major scale. To find the relative minor of its major scale, sing or play the major scale and then descend 1½ steps as follows:

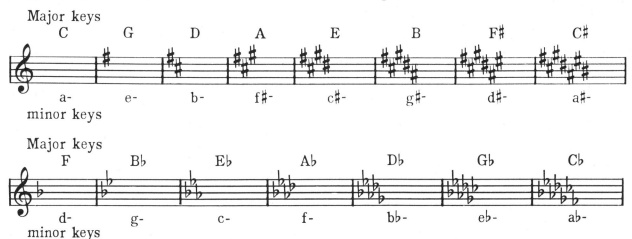

The minor scale is a hybrid scale. There are three forms: the *Aeolian minor,* also called the *natural minor;* the *harmonic minor;* and the *melodic minor* (note examples below). The harmonic form is usually used, as the name implies, when harmonies are involved. The melodic form has raised sixth and seventh degrees, or notes in the ascending scale, and the descending scale is like the natural minor, with lowered sixth and seventh degrees. For improvisation play, sing, and spell the three forms until you recognize their differences and their qualities become well established in your ear.

Aeolian or
Natural Minor   Harmonic Minor   Melodic Minor

raise 7th degree   raise 6th & 7th degrees ascending
                          lower 6th & 7th degrees descending

You can now enter the more inspiring avenues of improvisation; making a melody to a Psalm can be your first free venture.

EXERCISE 22 — How to Make a Melody Using a Psalm

This is your first "free" improvisation.

Feel the quality of the words, of a favorite Psalm.

1. Say the words first (as you might during a first reading).
2. a. Intone the words objectively (as you might to a listener). b. Almost murmur this Psalm, quietly, subjectively, almost to yourself.
3. Find the accented places. Gently tap out, or clap, or indicate with some movement that has meaning for you, the accented places.
4. Draw on paper or in the air the general line or curve that the words might take on as a melodic line.
5. Hum or sing the first line. Does it feel somewhat suspended? Somewhat like the question feeling? Does the next line arouse further expectancy? Where does the first cadence (close) arrive?
6. Commence with the first line again (not being concerned as to whether you repeat the exact melody of the first improvisation). Continue through to the end of the Psalm. Do not criticize or halt. Move on without holes in the time-space. It is understood that rests within the rhythm of the piece are desirable, whereas halting or hesitation impedes the flow of improvisation. You will find that where desirable, several sounds can be intoned on one syllable or word.

Soon flowing, inspired melodies will be improvised spontaneously, with favorite poems. Also you will improvise melodies without words, as well.

In contrast to free, improvised melodies, here are Beethoven's sketches, in six stages, for the opening theme of the adagio movement of the "Eroica" Symphony. See how studied and searching is the progressive development of this theme until Beethoven arrives at the version he finally used. Few examples could illustrate better the difference between "flash" initial improvisation and the results of a continued search for essence.

Beethoven's Sketches for the Opening Theme of Adagio Movement "Eroica" Symphony

VI Final Version

Adagio assai

CHAPTER V

Adventures with Unusual Scales

D O YOU know that there are hundreds of different scales? Certain scales are thousands of years old; on the other hand, new scales are constantly being developed. It is fascinating to experiment in this field.

Keep a firm grasp on the meaning of scale. The Oxford Dictionary defines it as "Series of degrees, ladderlike arrangement . . . sounds belonging to a key arranged in order of pitch . . . set of marks at measured distances for use in measuring or making proportional reductions or enlargement, rule determining intervals between these."

In the Western Hemisphere, most people are familiar with the major and minor scales. But the Oriental scales and some of those used in our folk and church music are quite different in their "measured distances"; the intervals between the tones are often different from the ones familiar to our ears.

For example, some of these scales include "quarter tones." The reader is asked to imagine the interval between one tone and another as being still smaller than our half step. Try to sing two adjacent tones with the smallest distance between them. If a "quarter tone" seems small, can you imagine even smaller intervals?

Leon Theremin, the man who invented the "ether-wave" instrument, had a device for measuring a hundred different degrees between a whole step, C and D. That, of course, was for scientific and musicological purposes. You need not attempt to sing these—at least not at present! I mention this research only to give an idea of the infinite possibilities in sound. Often, when you hear music of different races, it at first sounds "queer" or wrong to your ear. You must realize that the intervals may be different from those you are accustomed to hearing. Our occidental music sounds just as queer to an Oriental as his music does to us.

The following is an account of a scale built within a narrow range:

On the long-necked tambours the ligatures were located by almost entirely different principles—the most important being a step-by-step tuning nowhere else described in musical history: as applied on the 2-stringed tambour of Baghdad, this principle gave within a total compass of about a minor third a scale of eight notes.
　　　　　　　　　　　　　　　　　　—Charles K. Mead, *The Musical Scale of the Arabs.*

Here is a chant within a range of four tones.*

Kagura chant (Japan)   Range

"Listening for the first time to an Indian musician singing or playing," say Benjamin Britten and Imogen Holst in *The Wonderful World of Music,* "a musician of the West is more likely to feel bewildered; for the sound is utterly different from anything he has heard before. The tone seems harsh and the notes slide up and down . . . other scale degrees are flattened or sharpened according to what mode the music is in. 'A Certain' modal . . . scale needs a sharper F♯ and a flatter A."

Present day (Approximate) Indian Scales

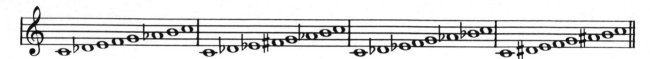

"The single melodic line of Indian music is never harmonized with chords; it is accompanied by elaborate drum-rhythms . . . There are no written notes; for the music gradually emerges as an improvisation.

"This elaborately organized variety which grows out of a few simple notes is the main characteristic of Eastern music. When an Indian singer and his drummer begin to improvise they are not plunging into the unknown and trusting to luck they will keep together. They are starting with a given *raga,* which is a fixed melodic formula appropriate to a particular time of the day and season of the year, and they develop it according to tradition, sometimes taking two or three hours over it, offering suggestions to each other and working up to tremendous climaxes with the freedom of confidence."

In India "dance programs list the scale (*raga*) in which the melodies are sung and the meter (*tala*) of the composition as if for a music program," Faubion Bowers observes in *The Dance In India.*

EXERCISE 23 — Wider Intervals

Just as there are intervals smaller than a half step there are also intervals larger than a whole step in some scales. A Hungarian scale has two places where the interval of a step and a half is normal. Try playing or singing C, D, E♭, F♯, G, A♭, B, C. The distance

* From "Oriental Music," Arthur Pritchard Moor, page 132, International Cyclopedia of Music and Musicians, ed. by Oscar Thompson; Dodd, Mead & Company.

from E♭ to F♯ is one and a half steps, and so is the interval from A♭ to B. Try improvising a melody using just the tones of this Hungarian scale.

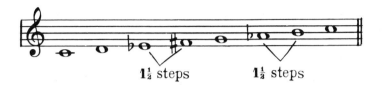

Do not try to translate it back to the major or minor scale. Let it preserve its own identity.

Your first improvisations may not sound like the "real thing" when using a new scale. Other elements besides the scale line must be included. One of these is rhythm. Imagination, as well as music as related to the dance, may also be considered. These ideas and experiences will blend in with the use of the special scale, and then you will be satisfied with the results. When working with the Hungarian scale, for example, you must imagine the Hungarian temperament, the country, its quality, and its characteristic rhythms in order at least to approximate the music language of that country.

You can probably see how it is possible to make an immediate improvisation "on demand" if you know the scale used in a particular country or culture and know something of the characteristic rhythms of the people, using your imagination in regard to their mood, emotion, costume, way of moving, dancing, gestures, and background. Of course research, travel, literature, and anything else you can add to your experience help to make the improvisation more inspired and more nearly authentic.

EXERCISE 24 — The Pentatonic Scale

To explore with other scales: The pentatonic scale (from *pente,* the Greek word meaning "five") can be found on the piano by playing the five consecutive black keys. You do not always have to play this scale on the black keys, but since these keys are spaced exactly according to the construction of the pentatonic scale, it is convenient to use them while experimenting with this progression.

Compare this scale with the sound of the major, minor, and Hungarian scales. Each of these has seven differing degrees, as compared with the five-tone pentatonic scale. How different in feeling they all are. You will soon recognize the differences and before long you will put the major scale (with its transpositions in all keys) in its proper place in relation to other scales of other cultures and concepts.

There is something very basic in the pentatonic scale. Otherwise, why do such diverse cultures as the Egyptian, the Chinese, the Scottish, the ancient Hungarian, the Javanese, the Balinese, the Negro, the American Indian, and the American folk use this scale as the basis for many of their melodies?

Here are some examples of these.

Arabic
(Egyptian)

Indian - Misra Jati (From "Oriental Music" by Arthur Pritchard Moor)
International Cyclopedia of Music & Musicians - Ed. Oscar Thompson - Pub. Dodd Mead

Negro: Nobody Knows de Trouble I See
Spiritual

American Indian: Pawnee (From "Pawnee Music," by Densmore, Bureau of American Ethnology, Bulletin #93, p. 90) "Power Is in the Heavens."

Chinese
"The Purple Bamboo"

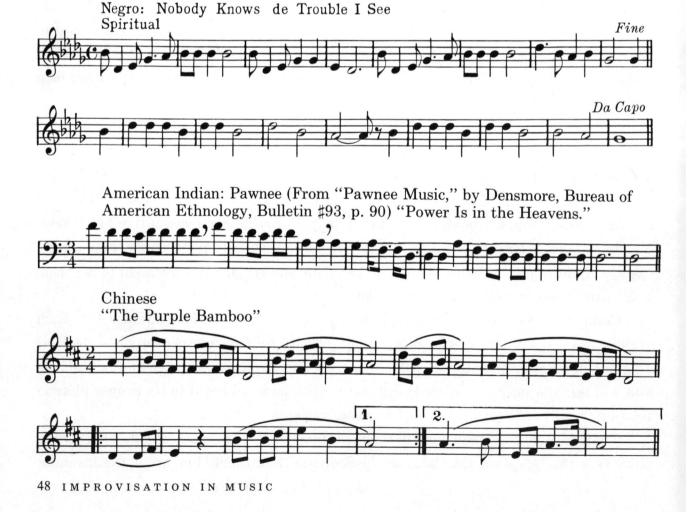

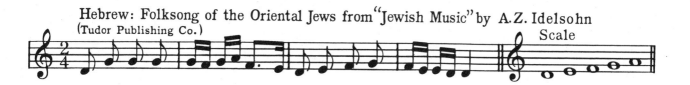

Hebrew: Folksong of the Oriental Jews from "Jewish Music" by A. Z. Idelsohn
(Tudor Publishing Co.)
Scale

American (Folk) from "Oklahoma" - "Jim Along Josie"
Scale

"Buzzard" American

Scale

Here is a selection of various unusual scales. Make improvisations on these, considering the rhythms, the setting.

Hungarian

1 step   ½   1½   ½   ½   1½   ½   1½   1½

Nine Tones

1½   1½

Chromatic Scale (all half steps)   Whole Tone   Four tone

Four Tone Scale

Arabian **Hindu** **Indian Raga**

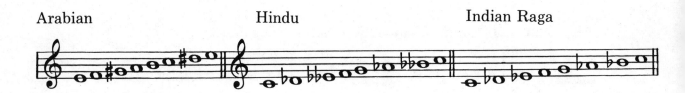

Egyptian

Irish **Pentatonic**

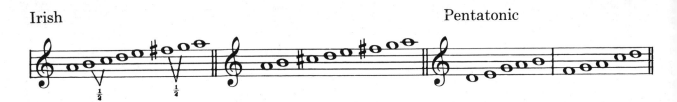

Modified Major Scale used in Jazz

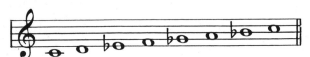

GREGORIAN MODES

Dorian **Phrygian** **Lydian**

Mixolydian **Aeolian (like natural minor)** **Ionian (like major scale)**

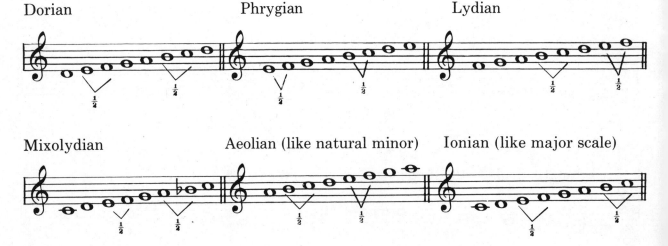

How to find the basic scale of a particular piece, for example, the pentatonic scale.

Scottish dance

Play the tune many times over, for the pleasure of it. Give it a good "look-hear!" Next, hold your fingers over all the notes you play, until all the keys that enter into this melody are depressed. You will see that no F or C appears, that D E G A B are the notes included, and these comprise the pentatonic scale.

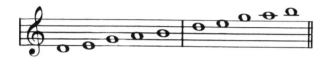

Now play the scale high or low, in various ranges, on the keyboard. Try playing the above melody by ear, including only the tones of the pentatonic scale, of course. Try transposing the whole piece to the black notes D♭ E♭ G♭ A♭ B♭. Start on D♭.

From special projects at a school where I taught, here are some results of the use of different scales. While working on plays about ancient Greece and the Crusades, the students used characteristic modes and made fairly authentic music to fit the period. Examples of their work in the Aeolian and Dorian modes are as follows:

Troubadour Song (Aeolian Mode)   *Peggy Heiman (age 12)*

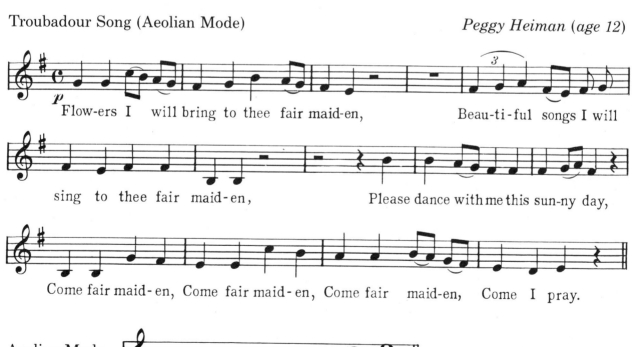

Flow-ers I will bring to thee fair maid-en, Beau-ti-ful songs I will

sing to thee fair maid-en, Please dance with me this sun-ny day,

Come fair maid-en, Come fair maid-en, Come fair maid-en, Come I pray.

Aeolian Mode

Drear-y days, Oh! This dis-mal cave. That one might come and happ-'ly

save us from e-ter-nal woe. Out-side the waves roll Phoe-bus sheds his light, but

we must stay to pay the toll of liv-ing in e-ter-nal night

Dorian Mode

Melodies using various scales, including some scales built by the students themselves, were made for recorder, flute, English horn, and other instruments.

Apply to these other scales the technique described in Chapter IV, melody-making for the major scale. These experiments will stir the imagination, encourage inventiveness and exploration, and help to enlarge one's musical horizon.

Two Pieces for Oboe *Thomas Scherman (age 14)*

EXERCISE 25 — How to Invent Scales of Your Own.

First plan a scale using the distance of an octave as the frame.

1. Use some half steps.
2. Use some whole steps.
3. Include wider intervals within the frame.

Here is a scale made up of half steps, whole steps, and, one and a half steps.

Following is a melody using this scale.

This is a scale of alternating whole tones and semitones.

Here is a scale with the distance of a third between each degree of the scale and the next. This scale covers two octaves.

Note that in this scale C is 1, E is 2, etc., and now listen to the difference in your improvisations.

After making up your own scales, then improvise, keeping strictly within the tones of the chosen scale (the "set of marks at measured distances"). Consider the setting, rhythm, etc., and "get going."

CHAPTER VI

How to Spark the Imagination

I, chanter of pains and joys, uniter of here and hereafter,
Taking all hints to use them, but swiftly leaping beyond them,
A reminiscence sing.

WALT WHITMAN

AS WE have noted, imagination is one of the six elements that blend to make a successful improvisation, the others being rhythm, melody, form, harmony, and counterpoint. What needs to be stressed first of all is that focus, discipline, and order are needed in the realm of the imagination. This goes counter to what many people think; there is a popular belief that the imagination is capricious and tends to wander. But there must be no sense of wandering in improvisation, as I pointed out earlier, and the improviser must acquire an understanding of the true imaginative factor in extemporaneous composing. No better way exists of grasping the nature of imagination than to compare it with fancy.

Put quite simply, imagination as it applies to musical composition connotes the exercise of creative power, whereas fancy suggests the play of more random, arbitrary, or capricious associations. Sir Leslie Stephen, English philosopher and critic, once said that fancy deals with superficial resemblances, whereas imagination deals with the deeper truths that underlie them.

There was much writing in the latter part of the eighteenth century and the early part of the nineteenth—the time incidentally of the golden day of improvisation—about the distinction between fancy and imagination. One of the best statements, and one worth pondering for a long time by the student of improvisation, was made by William Wordsworth. Wordsworth noted first that "fancy does not require that the materials which she makes use of should be susceptible of change in their constitution from her touch; and, where they admit of modification, it is enough for her purpose if it be slight, limited, and evanescent." But then Wordsworth declared roundly that "directly the reverse of these are the desires and demands of the Imagination. She recoils from everything but the plastic, the pliant."

Wordsworth's positive view is that "when the Imagination frames a comparison . . . the resemblance depend[s] less upon casual and outstanding than upon inherent and internal properties; moreover the images invariably modify each other. The law under which the processes of Fancy are carried on is as capricious as the accidents of things . . . but the Imagination is conscious of an indestructible dominion."

The practical question is how to spark the imagination, how to "trigger" it. Granted that the imaginative faculty of many people today has been neglected and is underdeveloped, how may we stimulate it to activity and growth? There is a means so simple that there is a danger people will not even try it. It is a means that I have encountered in the psychological laboratory and have repeatedly used with success in training young teachers of music. It consists simply in making an individual list of ideas for extemporaneous composition. That is not quite all there is to it. The list must reflect the students' interests. Some students are interested in moods and impressions; others are interested in dance movements or, like the poet Marianne Moore, in the motion of animals. Moreover, the ideas on this list are not merely nouns. The idea must always be a noun and an active verb, a subject and an active predicate—like "the tiger pounces."

Let me illustrate with a short list of very simple sentences. I shall put alongside it examples from the masterworks and folk music that have used ideas from the suggestive areas of the sentences.

Horse gallops	Schumann – *The Wild Horseman*
Ox plods	Moussorgsky – *Pictures at an Exhibition* ("Bydlo")
Sheep gambol	Castro – *Playful Lambs*
The mouse scurries	Folk song – *Three Blind Mice*
The pony trots	Folk song – *Hop, My Pony, Hop*
Leaves fall	Debussy – *Feuilles Mortes*
The cradle rocks	Brahms – *Lullaby*
The train chugs	MacCarteney – "Train Is Coming"
Gondola sways	Mendelssohn "Venetian Boat Song," *Songs Without Words*

Let me illustrate the imaginative process that was sparked by the first sentence of the list above: the horse gallops. This little sentence, of course, suggests movement. An experienced improviser would allow a place for contrasts, for suspense and climax, and thus move toward a more developed form. The sentence might lead you to imagine Pegasus flying through the air. In the instance of a seven-year-old boy who had spent a summer out West riding a little horse, the sentence gave him the idea of a colt galloping down the road, and here is his telling improvisation.

A-galloping

Tom Frank (age 7)

A gal-lop-ing a gal-lop-ing down the road I went — I saw a lit - tle colt — a rol-lick-ing a rol-lick-ing In a pad-ded green. He reared and turned up the road a-round the bend A gal-lop-ing he went — A gal-lop-ing a gal-lop-ing.

EXERCISE 26 — Sparks for the Imagination

Make a list of your own. Keep adding to it. Have it readily available so that if one subject is not immediately appealing to stir your imagination, another idea may do so.

Here are the first six ideas on a list a pupil recently gave me:

1. Kangaroo bounds
2. Leopard slinks
3. Moth flutters
4. Bell tolls
5. Monkey chatters
6. Clown mimics

Any device is to be valued if it acts as a springboard for your own ideas. For example, become aware of the rhythmic movement in seemingly inanimate objects . . . movement you might observe in the design of a rug, or in a nonobjective painting, or in a skyline . . . a rhythmic line that would be revealing to translate into melody and then develop.

One morning, while looking over some William Steig cartoons, I found myself so attracted by their keen satire and the subtlety of the psychology that I made eight music improvisations (at the same time recording them) of my impressions. Even the titles—"Members of a Culture," "Spiteful Little Man," "Man Who Feels Himself Imposing," "Possessions," "Victim of Flattery," "Ceremonious One," "Coy One"—were an instigation, and the cartoons contained as much movement as any dance. Later I notated the improvisations verbatim, played them often and arranged several for small chamber music ensemble.

Here is a suggestion that worked well for a young man pianist who had been offered a job to improvise for dancers. He had a good melodic sense and was keen about harmony, but he couldn't improvise on call. As a start I suggested that he try to play a succession of chords, allowing the succession to reach a climax and then drop down to the exhaustion point. Next, I suggested that he imagine a group of dervish dancers, who begin by turning slowly and gradually spin faster and faster as the music excites them to ecstasy. He made a convincing improvisation on this idea.

Sometimes a completely abstract sound or music motive, a series of chords, or contrapuntal movement will stimulate the music-making. Often we prefer it that way, as the more we enter into music language with no nonmusic "sparks," the nearer we come to "pure" music-making.

Jaques-Dalcroze made an epochal contribution to the art when he developed a system that allowed potential musicians to move, dance, conduct with the whole body, and including dynamics—before coming to the necessarily smaller confines of the piano, or other instrument, to proceed with the fingers. This was an essential advance over the limited and cramping practice of fingers first, "expression" last (or never).

I still meet students, usually adults, who say, "I'll learn the piece first, the notes, then the fingering, and then put the expression in last." But this is far removed from true imaginative musicianship and is never possible for improvisation.

One of the reasons that people are absorbed in watching baseball, football, a bullfight, the ballet, a conductor, is that they feel something more than a vicarious thrill. For the moment it is as if they become the pitcher, the dancer, the fighter. During this process something happens to the observer emotionally and physically, a response that the psychologists call "identification."

One can use identification consciously in relation to music-making. Here is where imagination enters. It is possible to recall an experience, set it up rhythmically, and relate it to music, without having to repeat either the physical act or even the sight of it. It is a little like the professional actor who recalls in his imagination the original mood, tempo, rhythm and action each time he performs on the stage. This is not automatic behavior. It is extremely conscious.

This ability to recall imaginatively needs to be developed and trained, especially in those who wish to make music a vital experience. The conductor of an orchestra understands this. But it does not prevent his producing a performance at white heat. He is in control every minute. The composer, the original "instigator," needs that white-heat stage (however outwardly he may be calm) to produce effective music. And the person with the desire to improvise music needs this drive as a generator.

Imagination in this sense, therefore, includes both real experiences you have had (and it is suggested that you recall them to enrich and enlarge your music language) and those you have not had personally but can imagine.

You understand, of course, that this is not necessarily a move toward "program" music—you are not attempting to translate a picture into sound. You are trying instead to carry over the rhythmic movement witnessed or being recalled imaginatively, alive and vibrant, into your music-making. This allows for the exploratory, inquisitive attitude, for the gathering of momentum, which carries a concept through to fruition. Neither "program music" nor "literary thinking" is our aim. Gradually we learn to think in musical terms, moving into the realm of pondering and feeling as the musician feels and thinks.

While on the subject of music imagination, a few words should be said about "expression" marks. The function of expression marks is to indicate what the imagination will have to supply in reading a piece of music. Expression has been defined as the name for that part of music which the composer was not able to commit to writing. The performer has to supply this unwritten part out of his own musical sense and emotion. This is a subtle part of the improviser's technique and must become part of his music vocabulary, not superficially, but with the inherent qualities implied in the terms.

For example, take the term "adagio," which indicates very slow movement. Imagine moving slowly forward, and at the same time moving as if with the feeling of being pulled back. Sing or play a music improvisation in the mood and pace that this Italian word suggests to you.

In the second movement of the "Eroica" symphony of Beethoven you have this mood and pace.

EXERCISE 27 — Expression Marks and Dynamics

Make improvisations in the mood and pace of each of the following expression marks, and dynamics. These qualities should be used imaginatively and not too literally.

EXPRESSION MARKS

Largo: dignified, slow pace

Grave: solemn, slow

Bravura (Italian for "bravery"): brilliance

Cantabile: singingly

Doloroso: (Italian for "painful"): sad

Dolce: sweetly

Giocoso: joyful

Allegro: quick and lively

Andante: walking pace

Animato: animated, with spirit

Appassionato: impassioned

Scherzo: light, humorous, quick

Gracioso: with grace

Prestissimo: very fast

Accelerando: gradually faster

Agitato: agitated, restless

Allargando: broader

DYNAMICS

pp – pianissimo: very softly

p – piano: softly

m – mezzo: medium

mp – mezzo piano: moderately soft

mf – mezzo forte: moderately loud

f – forte: strong, loud

ff – fortissimo: very loud

sf, sfz – sforzato: forced, suddenly loud

cresc. – crescendo: gradually louder ◁

decresc. – decrescendo, diminuendo: gradually softer ▷

Conduct or tap out the rhythm patterns of the following well-known music, particularly for the expression marks and the dynamics. This may be followed by listening to the records of the complete works.

Symphony No. 6, "Surprise," Haydn: second movement

Andante

Symphony in G minor, Mozart: first movement

Allegro molto

Symphony No. 7, Beethoven: second movement

Allegretto

Symphony No. 5, Beethoven: last movement

Allegro

Schubert Symphony ("Unfinished"): second movement

Andante con moto

Schubert Symphony in C: second movement

Andante con moto

CHAPTER VII

How to Listen

MY FIRST teacher in music pedagogy startled me with the blunt statement that people do not listen when they play. At the time I did not think it possible that people could play without listening. But I thought about my teacher's challenging assertion, and I wondered what was meant by "listening." Soon I came to see that to listen meant to be perceptive, to become aware of tonal relationships, and to reproduce sound that was first heard within. And I agreed that in this full sense of the word many people truly did not listen when they played.

One hears the melody easily enough, but it is necessary, for example, to learn to hear the bass, the root of a chord, and how that bass affects the melodic line and the harmonies. The awareness of the bass line helps one to build a solid foundation for all improvisation, allows for a wise choice of chords for accompaniments, and gives an insight into the playing of the music of the master composers.

Mlle. Nadia Boulanger, the great French musician and teacher, used to tell us to listen to the "inner part." I recall her analysis of a Beethoven quartet. At one point she had us listen carefully again and again to the effect of one tone in the tenor (viola) part, and how that affected the whole. We thus became aware of how one tone in an inner part, arriving at precisely the right moment, affects the texture of the sounds preceding and following. One short period of this kind of listening is worth hours of superficial "music appreciation."

Moreover, in improvisation one has to hear beforehand; one has to anticipate the approaching chord and to prepare rapidly for the final choice. In improvisation it is apparent that the ear must be ever alert, not for the sounds that have already passed or are just at the instant being played, but for sounds heard within, by the inner ear—sounds that must be listened for, detected, brought to the surface, and speedily reproduced on the instrument.

As extempore composers, of course we acknowledge that at certain points we allow our fingers on the keyboard free rein, we let them command a certain amount of play, occasionally even with frills or fireworks in cadenzas, depending upon our technical skills, and upon certain past experiences in improvisation which we like and tend to repeat with various transformations. Sometimes we are caught up by a series of sounds struck almost accidentally, and our zest for exploring them sends us along unforeseen streams.

Here is where training, control, and music experience support the character of the improvisation. One is constantly watchful against wandering, and it is the inner ear, the quiet listening, that really guides toward better musicianship.

At one time a professional pianist came to me for "ear" work. She had given concerts at New York's Town Hall, she was a teacher in an advanced conservatory, and she was producing artist pupils of high caliber. At this juncture she said that she had discovered that she didn't hear! She had been so busy with other aspects of her work that she had neglected listening. She had a good photographic image of the pieces she played and a brilliant technique. But she explained that the inner hearing that had been hers when a child had become buried by many layers of other activities. During our sessions she would sit quietly at the piano with eyes closed and work toward really hearing melodies and chord progressions.

Let me indicate an approach to the kind of work this pianist and I undertook in the art of listening. It has been found useful in the teaching of improvisation. We start by training the ear.

EXERCISE 28 — Training the ear

Play a low C or a chord or a broken chord on the piano, sustain it with the pedal. Listen to the sound, especially as it gradually recedes, and keep asking yourself, "Can I still hear any sound?" Listen until the sound has completely faded away. We should continually be in this state of alert, listening when we are playing.

EXERCISE 29 — Familiar Tunes

One of the first and most inviting steps in ear-training is to learn to pick out tunes by ear (on the piano or other instrument). You sing a tone and try to match it on the instrument. We call it "matching tones," as you try one tone and then another until you find the exact match. Gradually you gain a clear sense of tonal distances and relationships.

Make a list of familiar songs you like to sing. Choose an easy one. Then find the first tone; that is, sing a tone and match it on the instrument. Sing the next tone. Ask yourself (and this is an important distinction), "Does it sound up or down the scale from the first tone?" While singing the second tone, try for it on the instrument. Is it near or far from the first tone? If far, try a wide distance, a wide interval. If near, try the adjacent tone. You will soon learn to listen and to find the exact sounds with assurance. At the same time the satisfaction of playing "by ear" is yours.

After picking out familiar tunes and learning in this preliminary way to listen, you will begin to hear your own improvisations springing from within. You may sing or whistle them at first, and then recapture these beginnings of original tunes on an instrument. Then, if you desire, you may learn to notate and to develop them.

EXERCISE 30 — Color changes of one tone

Next, sing or play C. Add one tone above or below C. Listen to the changes in color of that C, as other tones are added to it. Make examples of two-, three-, and four-tone combinations with C sustained throughout.

Play and sing each C and listen carefully to the changes in feeling as other tones are added to it.

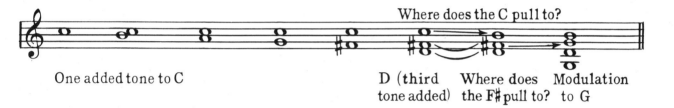

One added tone to C   D (third   Where does   Modulation
                                          tone added)   the F♯ pull to?   to G

Sing the C, while playing the chords slowly, and listen to the effect of the changes.

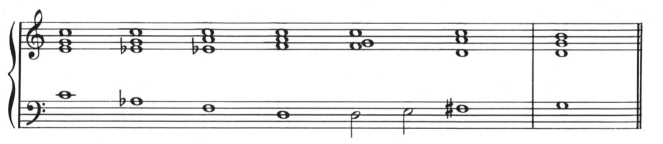

Sing C in the alto voice.

1. Sing C in soprano.
2. Play, bringing out the repeated tones on bass line.
3. Sing the alto line.

Continue building chords sustaining one tone on each degree of the scale.

EXERCISE 31 — Anticipation

There is a technique for listening ahead. Here are the essentials of it:

While playing a first chord, train yourself to hear the chord that is to follow.

Take a familiar hymn or patriotic song in which chords follow in close succession. While playing one chord, anticipate the sound of the following chord. Gradually hear two or more chords in advance.

Next, try a folk song. Anticipate the sound of the chord in the accompaniment that is to follow at the beginning of the next measure. Gradually train to hear a whole phrase ahead. (In folk songs the same chord is often repeated in several measures.) Then, even when the chords appear in broken-chord form, you will be able to anticipate approaching *whole* chords.

The First Prelude, in C major, from *The Well-Tempered Clavichord,* by J. S. Bach, serves as an excellent model. Play as written, in broken chords. While playing one measure, hear the next complete chord in advance. Gradually hear several measures ahead.

At this point we may well ask, How is it that we have become so sophisticated that we are taught to shun picking out tunes by ear? Isn't music primarily ear-hearing, and only secondarily seeing? We must remember that often the person with a "good ear" shows signs of special talent. Sometimes we teachers must refrain from introducing over-formalized instruction too soon with that type of person. Let me cite the case of little John.

"It's my ear," said little John in a most apologetic tone. "I can play by ear, but I can't read music. And when I try to read the notes, my fingers get all twisted."

John's mother appeared to be equally perplexed. Proud that her son was born with a good ear, she nevertheless remarked, "What can we do about his music? He won't practice along conventional lines, but he'll play for hours by ear. He likes to listen to records and the radio, and he often reproduces what he hears, but he won't practice, nor try to read music."

Why be apologetic about a good ear for music? Why should one be made to feel different because certain secondary processes (in this instance reading music and formal practice) appear to be more important? People are likely to hide basic attributes and their development in the background, while time, energy, and materials are lavished on the secondary values. This sometimes blocks the more important functions. Real talent may lie dormant. When that occurs, the individual feels unfulfilled and frustrated.

What is one of the most important elements in music-making? Surely the ability to reproduce sound with rhythm. Some say, "Only gypsies play by ear," but I have known other people who can play by ear and gain tremendous satisfaction from doing so. I have also watched those who have learned a few pieces only through study of the written music page and who cannot play anything by ear. As a result, the latter often feel limited in musical experience.

When John first began to try to read music, I noticed that he appeared blocked. On the other hand, he was ready to play practically the whole score of *Oklahoma!* by ear, with the correct chords; he had acquired this readiness through listening to the records and then transferring the sounds he heard onto the keyboard, chords and all. It was amazing. John was only eight years old, and his hands certainly were not large. Yet he could manage the rhythm, the melody, and even the exact chords, although scores like *Oklahoma!* are not composed of just elementary chords.

Of course, it is a great delight to the experienced musician to be able to read and play music at sight and to hear a score inwardly, even without playing it. I obviously do not deprecate the value of sight-reading music. Reading music is obviously important as a tool. But to impose reading and all the secondary techniques on a musical student, before he has built a strong bridge from his ear to the instrument, is to—well, to mix our figures, it is to put the cart before the horse. This is a delicate process, this building of bridges with intangibles. Here we have an innate talent, here we have an instrument, and here we have an eager learner. What often happens? We sit him down at the piano and teach him what middle C looks like on the page and piano, when he really would like to cover the keyboard with tunes, broken chords, and other inviting patterns. Many teachers now include the "ear" approach during lessons, if time permits. Where talent invites it, they are ready to help solve this problem, that is, when a forty-five-minute lesson with all of its other demands allows for this careful process. Of course, the ideal solution is to make music study as important as other subjects; and that may come someday.

The ideal way is through a careful balance of ear, eye, rhythmic feeling, speedy thinking, and alert response. One uses all these facets in the training for improvisation and for any music-making.

For John I finally made the bridge between his ear and reading in this way. We looked over the piano score of *Oklahoma!* for him to find certain chords he could not duplicate exactly by ear. We examined the printed music together, so that he could begin to see for himself the value and possible use of reading music. The written page was used for reference at first, to reinforce and support his growing musicianship.

Gradually, he came around to reading. He learned to read and play short pieces of Bach, Schumann's *Album for the Young,* and Bartók's (*Pro Deti*) *For Children,* among others, in order to become acquainted with piano literature, and followed through with accompaniments to Schubert and Schumann songs. We also concentrated on a certain amount of technique (working through improvisation). He learned to write music, one of the best ways to learn to read music is through writing it. Although his reading never was as quick as his ear, we did make a good connection from ear to eye, and he continued to grow, using his special talents. The ear way for him was far superior.

For teachers or parents another simple approach to careful listening and response, especially with children or with families, is the "Echo Game." The teacher sings several notes, like "Good Morning!" or "Hello," and the child echoes them. Then the child sings and the teacher echoes. Each child has a turn being the echo while standing or hiding some distance away.

Recently we had good results with listening and true pitch response in a children's class. Several of the children were not apt at carrying a tune, and one child was nagged by her older brother, who had a very keen ear. He'd say, "Janie, you're all wrong. You're not singing the right notes."

I know many grownups who, when children at school, were told that they were monotones. Some were told not to sing at all—"just mouth the words as if you were singing." This condemnation carried over to their adult lives, and as a result they believe that they cannot sing. With children, especially, it is important to avoid any remarks about inexact reproduction of tones, because often a child with a fairly good ear may be restrained from singing easily on true pitch for some unknown reason, possibly habit pattern, fear, tension, or lack of adjustment of the singing apparatus. Some people sing on pitch earlier than others. In Janie's case, while we played the Echo Game in class, I was careful to sing slowly and very clearly a "Hello," or "Good Morning," and to wait quietly for her echo. Each day there was improved pitch, until her true pitch was firmly established.

From Texas comes a folk song that makes a good Echo Game, from *American Folk Songs for Children,* by Ruth Crawford Seeger, published by Doubleday & Co.

By'm Bye

CHAPTER VIII

How to Recapture an Improvisation

IT WILL not, of course, be long before the student of improvisation encounters the "missing link" problem. One day he will get, so it will seem, the whole composition on the spur of the moment, but the next day there will be parts that he cannot remember— the missing links. Now it is quite possible to recapture an improvisation. There is an indirect way of going about this, but I think this may best be explained in a case-history form. Notice in the following story how Jack found the missing pieces of the improvisation puzzle.

Jack, an eight-year-old boy, was an odd little mixture. When he came for his music lessons, he often appeared contained and quiet but somehow excited underneath, with some new idea brewing, about music or airplanes or what not.

One day Jack decided he was tired of his music. He didn't want to practice at home. His mother urged and he resisted. She told him that he could not have lessons if he did not practice. Then she came to ask me what I would advise. I was sorry that she had threatened Jack with the usual formula, "No practice, no lessons."

Music lessons at first should not depend solely upon the daily practice period of a child. Occasionally, the child is working out something subconsciously, and forced routine practice might tend to bury rather than to nurture this subconscious work. And sometimes a child is just too weary of endless routines to wish to carry an added burden at the end of a school day. Sometimes he is just plain lazy, but we should give a child the benefit of the doubt until we discover the real causes.

I suggested that Jack take a holiday for a week, but that he understand that it wasn't because he had not practiced the previous week. One does not like to override a mother's directions to her own child. Yet it is sometimes important to do so if it protects and strengthens the child's own inner growing powers. Fortunately I was leaving town to give a program that week, and that made a good reason for the holiday. I prescribed a period of "let go" for Jack.

The next week he returned with a rather distant attitude. We started politely enough with the Couperin *Chaconne* on which he had been working, continued with technique and sight-reading, and concluded the lesson with the arrangement for piano of a

Beethoven theme (from the Trio, Opus 97) which we had made together from the original. However, very little of a spirited nature happened during that lesson, and he went away in the same distant state. I suggested a longer holiday, but he phoned during the week to say that he wanted to come for his next lesson.

Something was brewing. He had a new "make-up" piece (improvisation) coming along. He played the first theme, and then began to grope, to hesitate; he continued for a while, played the second theme, again hesitated, tried, went on, halted, came onto a third theme, and then stopped and said, "I went off. I had a nifty part. Yesterday it led up to the third theme by some mysterious way. It's baffling. Now I can't catch it." Jack continued. "I got the whole thing yesterday. Can't remember those parts now. There seem to be missing links. It's like part of a jigsaw puzzle. There are missing pieces. How can I find these?"

Now we got busy. We first made a record of the material as Jack had it then. It sounded like a person groping with an idea and seeking its outer expression. The boy was evidently hearing within himself, probably vaguely, the sounds of the music material which he had captured the day before (or it might possibly have been similar material, half formed). Next we made a record of the themes alone with silent spaces between them, allowing for about the time-space which Jack thought the episodic material would demand. Then we wrote his themes with the chords and all.

Next we examined several of the early Mozart sonatas and the Bach Inventions for the manner of treatment of episodic material. Jack read them and tried them out himself, and I played parts for him in exaggerated manner in order to bring out the feeling of the episodic material. We discussed all this quite thoroughly, comparing and relating themes, episodes, and cadences, too.

The next week Jack said he wanted the piece itself to start with the second theme. He had been working that way at home. Then he groped toward the third theme and finished with the first theme. (This made me realize once again that work may not be born in progressive, final form or order.) At this point Jack left his original work and continued with straight piano lessons, because his own "missing links" had not come through to his satisfaction.

The climax came two months later, when Jack came in shining with "Today I have lots of links." He went to the piano and played three or four good-sized episodes.

I said, "They are very good. Now what do they link? Which themes do they link?"

He said, "I think they're the missing links to my old piece."

We laughed. I asked him to play the episodes again, which he did very easily, and in a flash of memory one of his old themes came to my mind. We looked up Jack's themes in his music manuscript book. The missing links had been found—correct keys, range, rhythm. He played the whole piece through and even played it for a program that was given just for children.

There was a postlude. The next week Jack came and said, "I don't like it. I'm going to make another piece." Which he did! So goes the artistic temperament . . . satisfied, then dissatisfied with past accomplishments, and then on to conquer new problems.

This experience taught me many lessons. I became more acutely aware of the mysterious workings of the inner world, not only as manifested in the child, but also as basic to all creative work. For any age, a childlike attitude and tenacity of search are essential, and rewarding. Not all "creative" music-making needs to be great music that lasts forever. Through the *doing,* something genuine occurs which enhances all future music experience for the individual.

Suppose Jack had been urged to practice his regular pieces and exercises when he was feeling empty and tired, or suppose that he had quit his music at that time? Then he might never have broken through to his rich inner life.

With what might appear as a most indirect approach (and sometimes the way of working improvisationally does appear most indirect), the channel is allowed to open out so that, even months later, an original idea is recaptured—perhaps even enriched during its "waiting" period.

Persistent explorations with the masterworks feed the original music-making. Because Jack already had his themes, he needed to understand, through examining the master composers, how they made their links, their bridges, through episodic material. Possibly most rewarding, his playing of Mozart, Couperin, Beethoven, Bartók and others became proportionately more alive as he increasingly understood their values.

Although Jack's history may appear to be an isolated case, this situation does come up often in one form or another, especially with the more responsive music students. To those who need to recapture an idea, Jack's story exemplifies the general principle that applies to all of us: the *indirect* pursuit of an idea, the achievement of a state of release, and the eventual coming alive of the whole improvisation.

And here's how, step by step, we can go about recapturing an improvisation:

1. Do *not* try to catch the detail.
2. Try for the big sweep.
3. Relax.
4. Try to recall the original feeling or some association with it.
5. Recalling the rhythm often helps.
6. Make pitch pictures for the general line of melody.
7. *Try not to care.* (Prevents burden.)
8. If there are any specific particulars, search the masterworks.

CHAPTER IX

Building Forms

FORM GROWS out of rhythm. In the preceding chapters we have been building the simple music sentence, the four-measure group, and the question-and-answer (motive-and-complement), four measures balanced by four measures. Now let us advance further into the subject of form, or fluent design, in music.

We may define form very simply as the plan of construction in motion of a musical composition. Form is the shape of a piece of music; it is often referred to as the architecture of the piece.

A very brief historical sketch may serve to bring out the nature of form. Let us first consider primitive man as he begins to make his first music sounds. Perhaps his elements are a drumbeat and its rebound. From these, form emerged. How? Primitive man found certain satisfactions in what was almost a drone. To our ears his repetitive playing sounds monotonous. Perhaps it sounded so to some lone primitive music-maker. He may have become bored with the utterly repetitive. He longed for something different, something new—and he started to experiment with his drum. Ernst Ferand, the recognized authority on improvisation, has noted that musical utterances and improvisations, in their early beginnings, were practically simultaneous.

Our primitive began to chant along with his steady drumbeat. His tribesmen go off to battle. His drumbeats change from placid contentment to excitement and even to frenzy. The beat is persistent. Emotion rises with it. The beat becomes louder and louder, possibly faster, then gradually the sounds diminish to the end.

Primitive man had come upon a main principle of form, which is to avoid perpetual repetition at one extreme, and perpetual change at the other extreme. Form, it has been said, is a degree of change plus a degree of repetition.

We find that, as mankind advanced from the primitive stage, rhythm and music were emanating from the folk; we come upon the folk songs and peasant dances. Folk song and dance have had great influence on our present forms. The rondo form emerged—one in which the principal subject appears at least three times with contrasting material between repetitions.

Church music came to the fore. The church musicians were at first expressive through plain song, and then through the strict contrapuntal forms that prevailed in the sixteenth and seventeenth centuries. That was the time of Frescobaldi, the great organist, and Froberger, who were famous improvisers.

We know that Johann Sebastian Bach was a master of improvisation, as were various members of his family. In this remarkable family there were seven generations of professional musicians, making music for church and court. Bach's music language was so complete, and he himself was so well organized, that he evidently felt no need to experiment with new forms, but was entirely prepared to express his great universal art through already existing forms.

Besides his serious works—the great organ works, the Masses, the concertos, the cantatas, the fugues—Bach expressed the more playful moods when he composed music out of the dances of his day. His suites and partitas consisted of minuets, gavottes, bourrées, and gigues (jigs) expressing the spirit of the French, German, and English dances of the period. On Bach "family-days" they sang *quodlibets*. *Quodlibet* in Latin means "what you please." A kind of musical joke consisting of an "extempore juxtaposition of different melodies, whether sacred or secular, which were incongruous either in their musical character or in the words with which they were associated," as Groves Music Dictionary defines it. One of the best examples (page 189) is the thirtieth and last variation of the Goldberg Variations, where Bach uses two amusing German folk tunes as well as the main theme of this work for harpsichord.

But let us pass from history and theory of form to practical exercises in form.

EXERCISE 32 — Motive-and-Complement

Experience the question part as the swing forward, and the answer as the swing back, then tap out rhythmically.

EXERCISE 33 — Song Form (ABA Form)

The next longer form is the song form (ternary, or ABA form). In the diagram below take the A part (which is a question-and-answer) and then repeat this A part. Move on to the B section, and finally return to A section. Relate this to the rhythmic experience of the ocean wave, the vigorous bounce of the ball and its rebound, or the swing and its return.

Feel the A and the A repeated as the swing forward, and the B part and the return to A as the swing backward. You gather enough energy at the beginning of these thirty-two measures to carry you through. I can imagine that a well-trained trapeze artist knows this principle of motion and can give a sufficiently good impulse at the beginning to carry him through the desired number of swings backward and forward. The same principle applies here.

Tap out the whole ABA form, giving enough energy at the beginning to carry through the A, A repeated, the B part, and the return to A. This is how it works:

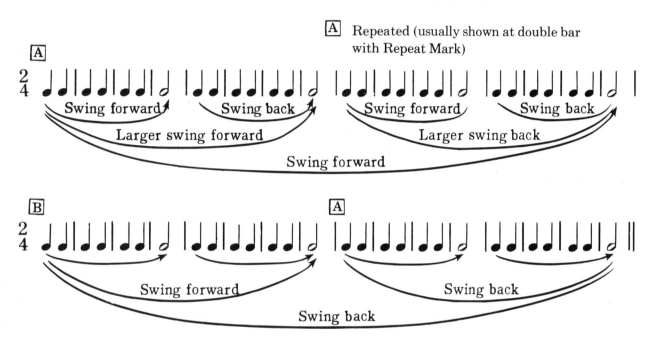

If a certain amount of energy remains at the end of an ABA form, a coda, which may be imagined as a "good-by" *after* the first "Good-by," may follow. Everyone knows how visitors go to the door, say a "Good-by," and then sometimes remain at the door for some time with a "That reminds me" before they say their final "Good-by." When at last they do leave, one may think, "Well, that was a pretty long coda." When you like a piece of music that you are making, and you still have enough energy left not to wish to drop it right away, you may produce a good coda.

When you begin to improvise your melodies in ABA form it is well to start and end the A section on the key tone. Let the B section commence and end on a tone *other* than the key tone—thus giving a feeling of expectancy and suspense. Then return to the key tone at the beginning of the final A section, and end on the key tone.

A useful outline to keep in mind for relating form to harmony is:

Start and end on the tonic chord (built on first degree of scale). A section

Start and end on the dominant chord (built on fifth degree of scale). B section

Start and end on the tonic chord. A section

Bear in mind that it is only the *feeling* of the tonic or dominant chord that you finally express. As you advance, you will find that the first section may not necessarily end on the tonic of the original key. It may end on the tonic of a related key. That also applies to the idea of commencing the B section on the dominant of the original or a related key. The dominant may be a related key to the original key.

It often happens that students can form a good first question-and-answer—and then wonder how to continue. One device for continuity is the use of contrasts. Contrast is a great aid to continuing an improvisation, an addition to the impetus the rhythm gives. Become increasingly aware of the many contrasts that you already feel in music. The table below should help one to recognize more contrasts in music.

CONTRASTS

Dynamics	loud (*ff*)	soft (*pp*)
Pitch	high sound	low sound
Range	high register	low register
Line	ascending line of scale (general)	descending line of scale
Modes	C Major	A minor
Keys	C	G
Rhythmic pattern	fast	slow
Mood	sad	gay
Voice	soprano	bass
Instrument	cello	flute
Line	curved	sharp
Touch	staccato	legato

If your A part is full, loud, and vigorous, perhaps in the second part, B, you will feel it softly, play it softly. Then you immediately have employed a contrast. While playing the A section, prepare and be ready to move right into a contrasting section as you enter the B part. Your music may not call for such sharp contrasts. Your music may need to flow more smoothly. The mood of the piece may need to be sustained without sharp contrasts. Or if it is a short piece, you will discover other ways of proceeding after the A section. Your innate sense of musicianship will guide you, finally.

However, studies in contrast are as much a part of your technique and discipline for vocabulary-building as are studies in rhythmic patterns, melody, and harmony.

One of the elements of contrast is tone color—timbre. To gain contrast, you might use the quality, the tone color, of the violin and contrast it with another tone color, like that of the cello. A feeling of orchestral quality often suggests the tone colors of different instruments. The piano can well suggest the timbre of other instruments. It is wise, therefore, to be aware of the element of timbre while listening and playing.

With children we can sometimes work out contrasts by getting them to think of imaginary creatures. A pupil of mine, for instance, made an interesting piece by using a conversation that grew out of the question-and-answer form. This boy was captivated by the idea of a conversation between an elephant and a goblin. Play *The Goblin and the Elephant* and you will see that his rhythm, the range on the keyboard, and even the story that he built with it have different dynamic qualities, different range, and obvious contrasts.

The Goblin and the Elephant
David Katcher (age 8)

A cave in the mountain is the scene of a Goblin Dance.

Near the finish of the dance a slow and ponderous knock is heard.

"Come in! Come in! Come in!" said the Goblin King.

In comes an elephant, he walks to the throne of the Goblin King and makes a stately bow.

What do you want? What do you want? said the Goblin King.

"I wish" said the elephant, "that I may be as light as a fly."

"No! No! No!" said the king
rather abruptly and angrily.

Please! Please! Please!
said the elephant.

No! No! said the king
more angry than ever.

The elephant moves slowly and sadly away.

As the Goblin Dance begins again.

Here is a rondo form (ABACA). It is a peasant dance made by a twelve-year-old boy.

Peasant Dance

Henry Morgenthau III (age 12)

Allegro

Fine

mezzo

D.C.

TRIO

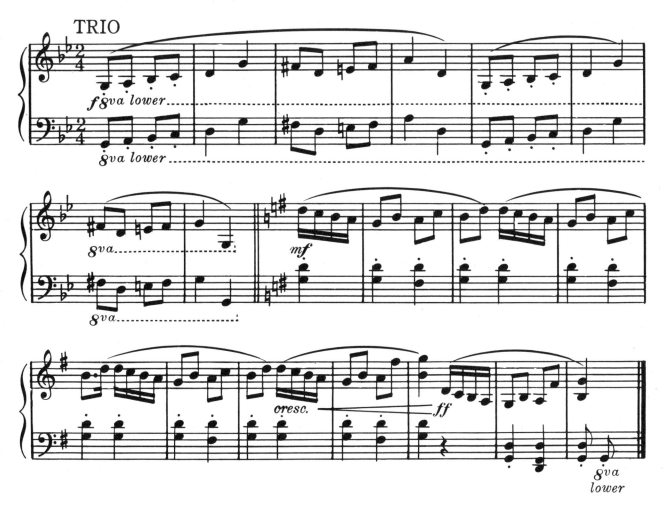

He imagined a group of peasants meeting on a village green during a holiday. They are dressed in their finery, the rosy-cheeked girls with wide embroidered skirts, bright ribbons in their hair, the men in their Sunday best, wearing high shiny boots. All are feeling very gay and ready to dance.

Now they begin.

A   All dance together. Key of G major.

B   Girls dance in the center while the men stand in an outer circle and clap. Key of E minor (relative minor).

A   All dance together again. Key of G major.

C   Men dance alone (showing off their tricks, their high boots). Girls in outer circle clap. Key of G minor (tonic minor). Low register.

A   All dance together again. Coda to end. Key of G major.

EXERCISE 34 — Rondo Form

Start your own improvisation of rondo form, using the above description as a springboard. First feel the form rhythmically. Get the sense of the whole before you start. This longer form is as much a unit of impulse and reaction as the question-and-answer.

The improvisation of rondo form can be extremely useful as a springboard to other forms of music. It is a simple form, rather spread out, and quite easy to experience. After trying out the contrasts in A and B and C, and the continuity through the return to the A section each time in this form, make the shorter song form: ABA.

It is as if you made a wide survey, viewed the field, and then gradually became more discriminating when you approached the shorter, ABA form.

SONATA FORM

One becomes much more discriminating in the sonata form, in which careful choices of a first theme and a second theme are made with a completely planned and thought-out form. However, the same principle of ABA obtains, the A being exposition, B development, and A recapitulation (the return).

A			B	A		
Exposition		:	*Development*	*Recapitulation*		
a	b		a b	a	b	
tonic theme	dominant theme	dominant key (codetta)	related keys	tonic	tonic	tonic (coda)

FUGUE

The fugue, the most precise and exacting form, is very carefully framed, without a waste of a note. Expressed through one theme, the fugue is the acme of musical form. Whether or not you arrive at the improvisation of a fugue, fughetta, or the less involved invention, you will nevertheless want to discern the wonderful architecture of this form.

Your own experience in the improvisation of the larger forms will follow in the degree that your interest allows you to spend time and to focus on this subject. Knowing the principles of form will influence all your improvisations, however simple or complicated they may become.

FANTASIA

The fantasia provides a good link between improvisation and written composition. In his *Essay on the True Art of Playing Keyboard Instruments,* C. P. E. Bach wrote:

A fantasia is said to be free when it is unmeasured and moves through more keys than is customary in other pieces, which are composed or improvised in meter. These latter require a comprehensive knowledge of composition, whereas the former requires only a thorough understanding of harmony and acquaintance with a few rules of construction. Both call for natural talent, especially the ability to improvise. It is quite possible for a person to have studied composition with good success and to have turned his pen to fine ends without his having any gift for improvisation. But, on the other hand, a good future in composition can be assuredly predicted for anyone who can improvise, provided that he writes profusely and does not start too late.

VARIATION

The variation form is presented in detail here because it is one of the most inviting forms for improvisation. Its many possibilities may be used as models toward improvisation, for it is carefully framed, formed, and keeps to the one-theme structure. There is little chance for wandering.

A couple of definitions are in order:

Variation:
Any extended composition in which the successive sections of the compositions are each derived more or less directly from the theme. The writing of variations was one of the earliest means adopted for producing an extended composition, and has continued to attract the attention of composers until the present time.

Passacaglia:
Originally an Italian or Spanish dance similar to the chaconne . . . The music of the passacaglia is constructed on a ground bass, but the theme may be transferred to an upper part and may be decorated.

From A Dictionary of Music, by R. ILLING

Variation allows for cumulative experience. You start with a theme and add one experience after another, increasing in intensity (through changes of either patterns or tempi); you finish with a feeling of expansion, climax, and resolution.

The passacaglia has been chosen here for illustrative purposes because it is constructed on a chord theme in the bass and because it is essential to *listen* to music from the bass up, the foundation of the structure, rather than to listen from the melody (soprano part) down.

In a theme with variations, only the bass is really important to me . . . It is the firm ground upon which I build all my floors. Whatever I do with the melody is a play or an ingenious game. But it is on the given bass that I invent my new melodies. It is here that I really create.

JOHANNES BRAHMS to Dr. A. Schubring in 1869.

In a passacaglia, you are bound to listen from the bass up. All of your improvisations will be helped tremendously as you make your own experiments, using this passacaglia as a model.

It is exciting for all improvisers, especially when built up in convincing fashion as in this inspired passacaglia by Handel from his Seventh Suite.

EXERCISE 35 — Directions Toward Relating Foregoing to Your Own Improvisations.

1. Memorize the bass.
2. Listen carefully to the chord sequence.
3. Notice the sequence in the bass, and the cadence (close) at the fourth measure. Observe the wonderful economy achieved within this four-measure phrase. Later you will choose your own chord sequence.

The first announcement is the chord theme in the bass, with the intervals of thirds and sixths in the right-hand part, in the dotted-note rhythmic pattern.

Variation I. The chord theme is in the right hand. Compare the similar dotted-note pattern of the first expression (above) with the pattern included in this chord theme (below). Note the scalewise motion in the left hand. The scalewise pattern repeats in sequence.

Direction: Devise sequence patterns in the left hand. 1 2 3, 2 3 4, 3 4 5, etc.

Variation II. The measures in the second part are an inversion of those of the first part. That is, the right hand takes (an octave above) what the left hand had in measures 1 through 4, and the left hand takes (two octaves below) what the right hand had before, so that the parts are "inverted."

Variation III. This has the same right hand as Variation II, with a stronger bass that reinforces the theme.

Variation IV. Now you come to the triplet (scalewise) figure in the right hand. Compare the preceding eighth-note figure with the feeling of the triplets. The chord theme in the left hand is reversed in the last four measures.

Variation V. The chord theme is in the left hand. The right-hand rhythm is the same as the first expression of the theme, using the descending G-minor scale.

Play this scale. 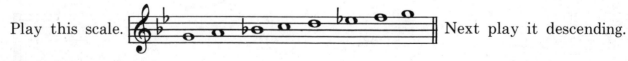 Next play it descending.

Next clap the dotted rhythm.

Play the descending scale in the above pattern, Variation V. First, starting on G, then starting on F, then, starting on E♭ in sequence. Remember this idea for your own improvisation of variations. Play any scale. Form a sequence, using part of a scale.

Example: 1 2 3, 2 3 4, 4 5 6, etc.

Variation VI. The chord theme is in the left hand, sixteenth-note scale passage with the inversion in the last four measures. Notice how cumulative the variations are becoming. Each one has more drive, more force, than the preceding ones. Compare the dotted notes, eighths, triplets, and sixteenth-note patterns.

Variation VII. This is another device for improvisation.

Examine the right-hand part. Note the way Handel plays on the return to the same note while otherwise moving scalewise. Play the B♭ scale descending.

Do you see how the pattern works? Experiment with this idea.

Variation VIII. Here is the first change of harmonies. Note that the chords descend chromatically, that is, in half-steps rather than scalewise.

Variation IX. Play as chords. Then experiment with various broken-chord patterns.

You are free to experiment with your own versions of broken chords. Ingenuity is invited.

Variation X. This is a coda. First play it as chords, then break the chords as written. It was the custom of the day of Handel and Bach to write successions of chords and allow the musicians to improvise broken-chord arrangements of their own.

Although there is decided discipline in making oneself remain within the given frame of a traditional form, nevertheless when we make a good improvisation, we are more concerned with inherent qualities and with how the work opens out from an inherent center of feeling than we are with the external shape of the music.

But while searching for and finding orderly methods of presenting ideas, so that symmetry, variety, and design fall into place, we at the same time are stretching the boundaries, until any sense of restriction or even suggestion of static form vanishes. Finally, form becomes so pliant, so plastic, that there is a constant sense of renewal—new life.

Then out of the improvisation itself the form grows organically, influenced by the theme, or by the pure palette of sound, of tone color, while the music elements flow through it.

Sometimes the form grows out of the emotional content, which is similar to a drama in feeling, in the sense of presenting characters and relationships between them, and in action toward a climax and then the moving toward the closing scene. (It is interesting to note that in graphs of music themes, the proportion of the rise to the fall is often three to one—similar in miniature to the three acts of a play rising to the climax, with the fourth act moving to the resolution.)

On occasion one gets a quick flash of the whole form while the improvisation is in progress. This may occur early in the improvisation. This is where intuition (call it inspiration if you like) takes over.

CHAPTER X

Free Counterpoint

FOR CERTAIN cultures, music expression through a single line of melody, either for singing or for a solo instrument, is considered to be a complete and satisfying experience. But it is often a natural step forward to experiment with music for two voices. It is logical then to introduce "free counterpoint," here in two parts (that is, two voices) before we take up the subject of harmony.

In the early days of written composition, when the idea of the practice of the art was to write down an existing plain-song melody (or *cantus firmus*) and against each of its notes to write another note for the accompanying voice, the two voices thereupon proceeded together at the same pace. A single part, or voice, added to another is often called, even now, a "counterpoint" to the second, but usually the word is given the general meaning of "the combination of simultaneous voice-parts, each independent, but all conducing to a result of uniform coherent texture" (W. S. Hadow). The Latin of it is *punctus contra punctum,* "point against point," or "note against note."

Counterpoint is the very essence of music expression. Consequently, the ability to manage at least two individual lines of sound, to maintain two parts at once, gives decisive and added power in improvisation.

Like two dancers moving independently, yet with the same purpose and continuously aware of each other, the two lines of sound sometimes play against each other, sometimes play together, sometimes support and sometimes alternate the movement.

This two-part work is extremely useful, particularly when you begin to explore its possibilities. The student is urged to discover all the possibilities, try all the combinations, and experience many variations within this seemingly simple two-part material.

Later one will learn to manage three or more individual lines. The great improvisers have been able to control four or more voices simultaneously, playing in contrapuntal movement, in form, and with inspiration. Johann Forkel has noted of J. S. Bach's improvisations that

He would start with a prelude, followed by a fugue in all registers. This could be alternated by a trio, also by a four-part counterpoint or a choral prelude. He finally concluded with a new fugue of highly complicated character.

In our discussion of counterpoint, we shall make use of graphic illustration—our graphs will illustrate ideas for improvisation; they will convert ideas into visual patterns as an aid to carrying out these ideas in aural, musical form.

In a much more simple and direct way than music notation allows, the complete, flowing form, the pitch, the duration, and the relationship between the two or more voices can be shown clearly in a graph. As you use the graphs, think of two independent voices, related, weaving a texture while each voice maintains its own identity.

In all of the graphic illustrations given below, time moves horizontally from left to right as in music notation, and a higher position means a higher note in pitch in the same general way. Instead of disconnected music notes, however, a continuous line is drawn which provides a kind of flowing silhouette or line drawing of a melody.

The difference between a quarter note and a half or whole note is merely one of length of horizontal line. Where there is a rest, there is a measured gap of the same length of time value.

Each horizontal square equals the shortest note value of the particular piece. A move from one square to another above or below it represents a half-step in pitch.

In using a graphic illustration, first gain a general sense of the line movement by following the two lines at the same time. For example, see how the alternate movement looks. Try to feel the general rhythm of it. Alternate movement can be compared to a game of tennis—first one player serves, then the other returns the play, and then they volley back and forth, always being aware of each other.

The sight of two lines, converging and moving apart, can be quickly related to contrary motion in sound.

See how parallel motion is shown clearly, linearly; while watching the lines, improvise the two-line music, not one note for each graph square, but only for the general line. Do not feel uneasy about the first rough results. As you become thoroughly familiar with the basic materials, your improvisations will gain conviction.

EXERCISE 36 — Alternate Movement

Since alternate movement is so natural and easy to feel in counterpoint, we shall begin with this type. The voices take turns at being active, and then at being comparatively passive and sustained. Where one voice (one part) has a sustained tone the other has more movement. This is further enhanced with a tie (over the strong beat). Think of a tie as a "suppressed accent."

Before playing, tap out the two rhythms with two hands on a table. Count aloud. Be sure to start on the up-beat. Keep it moving.

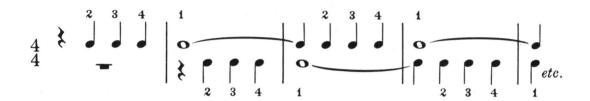

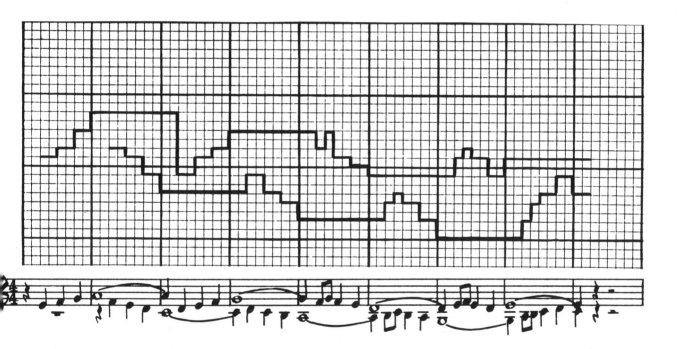

After you gain the basic feeling in quarter notes, include various rhythmic patterns. Next, replace the ties with rests.

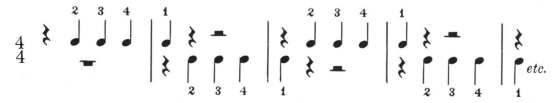

EXERCISE 37 — Contrary Motion

1. Start with the two thumbs on middle C and then move in opposite directions.

2. Start with C's, two octaves apart, then move the voices closer together, then away, forming a design in sound. Contrary motion is sometimes called "reflection," which might suggest thinking of the outline of a mountain and its image in a lake. That gives you a pictorial representation of contrary, or opposite, motion.

Before making too studied an improvisation, feel the general, large sweep of the movement.

Try pitch pictures, or graphs, and then try translating into tones, linearly, the general shape of your line pictures. Play with it freely, at first.

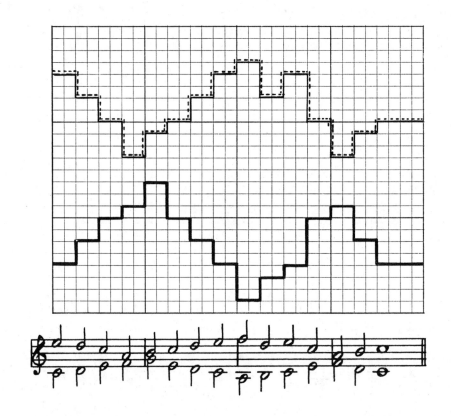

For a good example of contrary motion see the Bartók *Mikrokosmos,* Book I, No. 12.

EXERCISE 38 — Parallel Motion

With your two index fingers, play the interval of a third. Start on C and E. Ascend (as in the example in the graph), then descend, then ascend, descend, and end on C and E. Listen carefully to the progression in thirds.

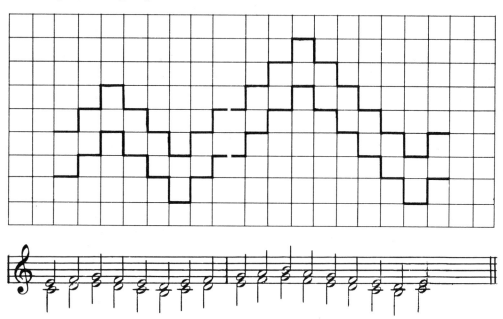

Next try the different intervals in parallel motion.

For 2nds, start on CD, then DE, EF, etc.

For 4ths, start on CF, then DG, EA, etc.

Listen and decide which you like best. Do you like 2nds, 3rds, 4ths, 5ths, 6ths, 7ths, octaves (8ths), 9ths, 10ths, in parallel motion?

Inversion and Expansion of Intervals

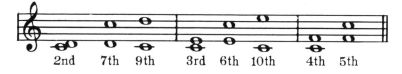

2nd   7th   9th   3rd   6th   10th   4th   5th

Notice that the interval of a 7th is a 2nd inverted;
the interval of a 9th is a large 2nd;
the interval of a 6th is a 3rd inverted;
the interval of a 10th is a large 3rd;
the interval of a 5th is a 4th inverted.

Therefore 2nds, 3rds, and 4ths with their inversions comprise all the necessary intervals.

Except for experimental purposes, I do not especially recommend the *parallel* movement in 2nds, 4ths, etc., at this time, but at least one should be ready to experiment with these intervals before settling down to the present so-called consonant ones. In the ninth and tenth centuries, progressions of either parallel 4ths or 5ths, called "organum," were considered consonant. Now these progressions are theoretically termed dissonant. Children accept many varieties of so-called dissonant sounds after hearing them often over radio and TV. We find many inviting qualities emerging today, particularly in combination with other intervals and timbres, as we keep an "open ear."

Considering the interval of the third as the most consonant interval (to our present ears), we shall build on that as the basis for this two-part work. This will also include the 6th and the 10th.

Try parallel 3rds, then 6ths, then parallel 10ths, then combine 3rds, 6ths, and 10ths. Play a series of 3rds, open out to 6ths, then open out to 10ths. Move into the 6th within the range of the 10th, and the 3rd within the range of the 6th or 10th.

EXERCISE 39 — Leaning Tones

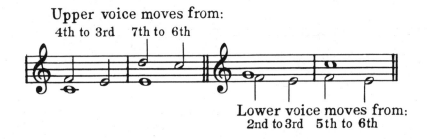

Feel the pull of the upper voice forming a 4th with the lower voice, and pulling from the 4th to form a 3rd.

Now hear the 7th pull to the 6th.

When moving the upper voice be sure to sustain the lower voice. Listen to the lower voice, particularly to its change of character as it sustains the movement of the upper voice and participates in the change from a (more or less) dissonant quality to one that is consonant.

The 5th can be considered as a consonant interval (not needing a resolution) or as a "mild" dissonant moving to the consonant interval of the 6th.

EXERCISE 40 — Figuration

Taking the scale in long notes in the lower voice, let the upper voice make a scalewise design above it. Then reverse, let the sustained movement be in the upper voice and the design be in the lower voice. Then combine.

Tap out various rhythmic patterns, letting one voice sustain longer notes while the other voice has more rapid movement.

Imagine two dancers. One takes long, slow strides, while the other takes short, running steps, varied by different patterns. Then they reverse their roles, the first dancer taking the faster movement, making decorative patterns around the slow strider, while each nevertheless maintains her own identity, though constantly aware of and gracing the partner's movement.

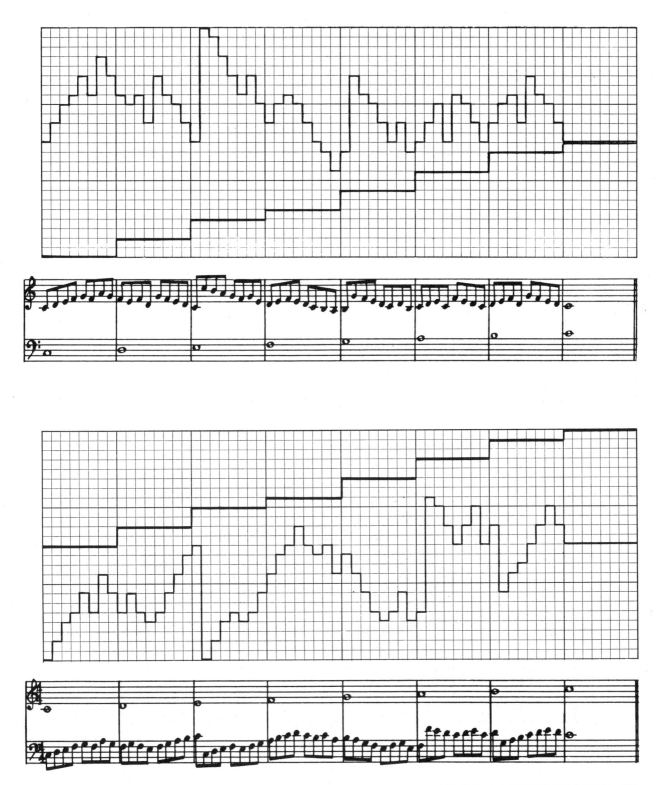

EXERCISE 41 — Combinations

Now you have five different types of free counterpoint to work with. Horizontal lines represent units of time. Vertical lines represent pitch.

1. Alternate movement (with ties and rests)

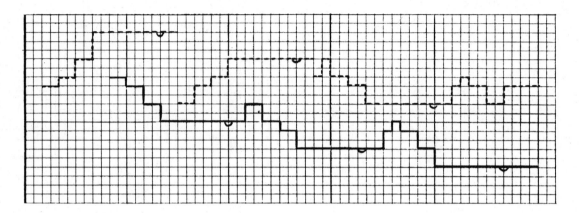

2. Contrary motion (also called Reflection or Opposite motion)

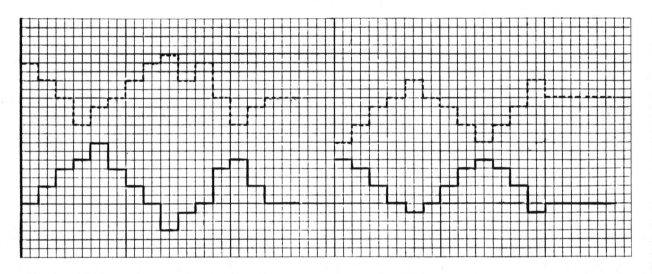

3. Parallel motion (in 3rds, 6ths, and 10ths and Combinations of 3rds, 6ths and 10ths)

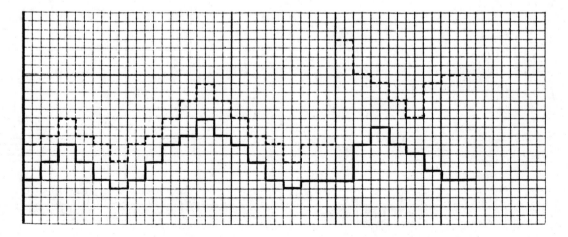

4. Leaning tones (Tension to Relaxation: 4th to 3rd, 7th to 6th, 2nd to 3rd, 5th to 6th)

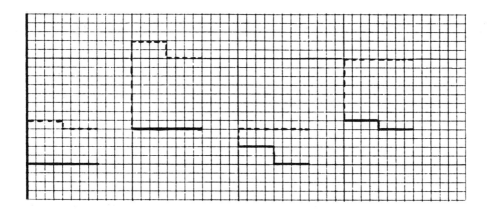

5. Figuration (Upper voice, Lower voice, Combination)

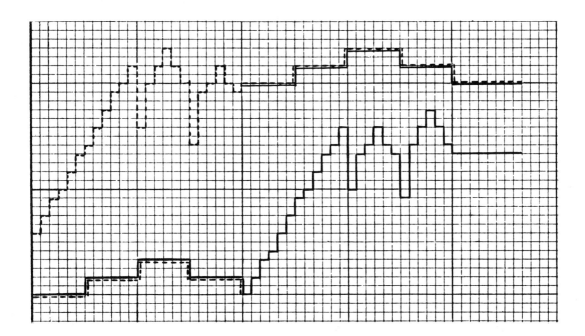

At first, watching the graph lines *while you improvise* helps to remind you quickly of the movement of the two lines and their relationships.

Keep these five types all in mind and at your fingertips so that you can combine them at will. First, combine any *two* types, then try combining *three,* etc., until you feel completely free with the movement of all types in two-part work.

After gaining independence with each type, begin to combine them. Feel the rhythm before improvising. There are endless possibilities. Cultivate agility in your thinking and feeling about the forming of combinations. When you think you have exhausted the field, it is time to start exploring and digging for richer material.

At this point I should like to offer proof of the efficacy of the graphic approach. While working with a young man who was actively interested in improvisation, I found that the question of free counterpoint versus strict counterpoint (noted below), particularly as related to improvisation, was a very live one. This student was quite free in the practice of harmony, but he had never studied counterpoint.

I first explained the processes of strict counterpoint: the use of the *cantus firmus,* the "fixed song," which is given in long notes, one to a measure, and employed as a basis upon which the student carefully chooses and adds a second part: first one note to each measure, then two, three, four (then sometimes six or eight notes). Then the student learns how the tie is carefully worked out, producing a studied syncopation to one note of the *cantus firmus.* Each of these species is first worked out on paper, practiced separately, and then combined. Later three, four, or more voices are added to the *cantus firmus.* Strict rules have been formulated, based on the vocal practices of the Renaissance, a period whose purity of line and standards have rarely been surpassed.

My student and I then compared this sometimes entirely theoretic study of strict counterpoint with the approach to free counterpoint, taking into account our present keyboard instruments, which are recognized as an excellent medium for improvisation. Too, as an added impetus to pianists, contrapuntal thinking and action can be expanded with exciting results to include harmonic play.

The comparison between strict and free counterpoint was not, of course, meant to disparage or discourage the study of strict counterpoint. For the serious student who plans to compose music, no study is more rewarding in the long run. Too, strict counterpoint, as taught at present, leans toward a freer approach. However, a good course to follow for the student who is less ambitious toward written composition and has a leaning toward improvisation is, astonishingly enough, a study of the works of J. S. Bach. Commence with the short dances in his *Notebook for Anna Magdalena Bach,* composed for his wife, pupils, and children. Then introduce yourself to the two-part Inventions, the short Preludes and Fugues, and the dances from his French and English suites and his partitas. (Bach made music of the dances of his day.) Finally and always comes the lifetime study of what the musicians call their "Bible"—the *Well-Tempered Clavichord.* This provides a fine balance and discipline, and removes any tendency to wander in improvisation.

Here is an inspiring example of two-part counterpoint, the opening of the presto movement of the Bach Flute Sonata No. 1, in B minor.

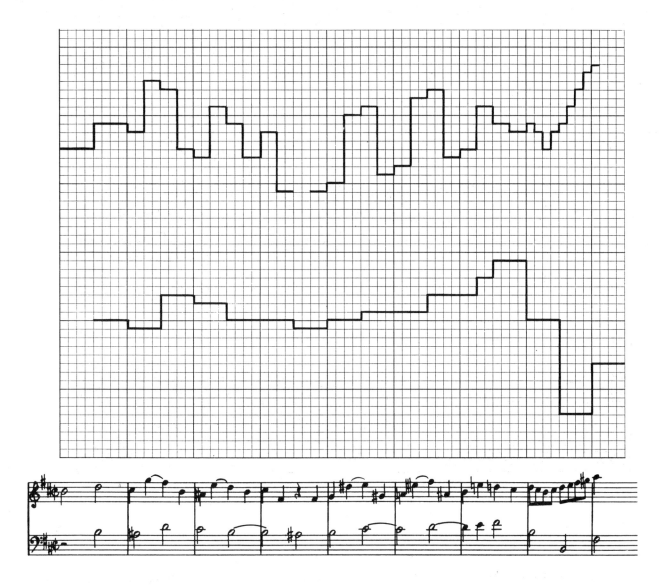

You may even find yourself pursuing a course in today's way with strict counterpoint after further insight and exploration.

When the young man began to experiment with free counterpoint, and after he had tried the five types separately, I asked him to try to combine them all. He floundered somewhat until I showed him the line sketches, the graphic illustrations. As soon as he looked at these, and kept on looking at them, although there was just a brief sketch of each (in two lines in two colors originally), he proceeded to improvise freely, combining and maintaining the two strands of melodies without the previous hesitation.

Considering that he had never had any previous study in counterpoint, his first day's experiments were exceptionally good. We made a tape of his improvisations so that he could hear and gradually become more discriminating in his choice of material.

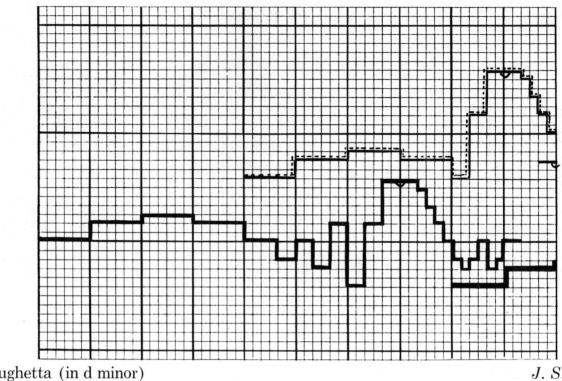

Fughetta (in d minor)   J. S. Bach

This experience of the young man proves that the graphic approach is an aid to the understanding of how two bodies (two dancers, two lines, two strands, two voices), moving independently within the law, can produce good, integrated improvisation. This was later followed with studies, including the visual, of three- and four-part material. See the D-minor Fughetta of Bach and graph for three-part material.

Counterpoint is generally reserved for the musically advanced scholar. Free counterpoint, however, provides an excellent approach to linear movement far earlier in one's musical experience than is usually thought feasible.

After gaining a further sense of the linear approach, begin to make your own graphs— or commence with more free line drawings and then continue by making precise graphic illustrations. When possible, sing each line as you draw it. Later you will be able to sing one line and hear the second line at the same time.

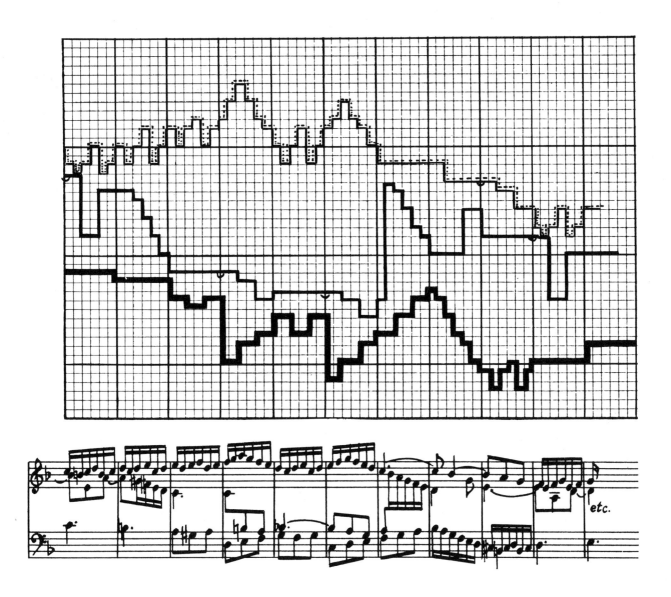

For making precise graphs, let each graph square moving horizontally represent one unit of time. Let each square moving vertically represent one unit of pitch (a half step).

EXERCISE 42 — *Die Meistersinger* Overture

In the overture to *Die Meistersinger* there are five themes expressed. In the excerpt below, three of the themes are expressed at the same time.

Try playing two of them together at first:

     1. omitting the middle line

     2. omitting the lower line

     3. omitting the upper line

Next, sing one theme and play the other two. When you listen to a record of this overture, you will hear that the "Love Confessed" theme is strongest at this point, while the other two themes are submerged.

Three themes from the *Die Meistersinger* overture   *Richard Wagner*

Listen to the difference between the "Meistersinger" theme played along with the other two themes ("Love Confessed" and "The Banner") and how that same theme sounds when played together with that of the "Toreador Song" from *Carmen*.

Here we can only make mention of a form of counterpoint called the "Canon." A simple example is "Three Blind Mice"—a round—in which one voice starts the tune and several measures later another voice commences and takes the identical tune while the first voice continues on.

Two examples follow:

Canon from the Symphony in D Minor, first movement   *César Franck*

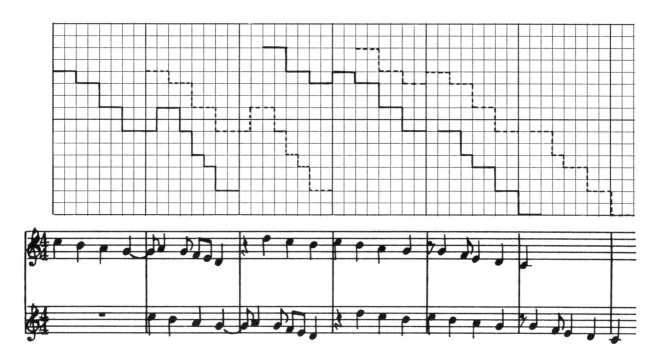

Here are two versions of a two-voice piece, in $\frac{5}{4}$ meter, and based on the following scale:

Note that in the second version the soprano line remains the same, and in the bass line there are changes in rhythm and phrasing.

EXERCISE 43 — Combining Free Counterpoint with an Unusual Scale

Choose a scale out of those in Chapter V, "Adventures with Unusual Scales," or form a new scale; decide upon the meter and make use of the combinations indicated graphically to design an improvisation of your own.

We shall resume the discussion of free counterpoint in chapter XIII, where these techniques are expanded and applied to combine with harmonic progressions for "on-demand" improvisations.

CHAPTER XI

Harmony and Improvisation

IN THIS and the three following chapters we shall take up the subject of harmony—
the art of combining sounds into chords in succession and treating them according
to certain laws. Adolf Weidig, in *Harmonic Material and Its Uses,* reminds us that
"harmony deals with tones, their relationship to each other . . . and their combinations
into chords. 'Harmony' in a historical sense is limited," he says; "in fact, it is reducible to
the three elements—tonic, dominant and subdominant. In the new conception these
elements must be considered as functions—i.e., every combination of tones into chords
produces the effect of one of these elements."

While the underlying laws of harmony are constant, what we may call the rules are
somewhat flexible and vary with period styles. Even dissonance and consonance are relative, for what sounds dissonant to one generation or for one purpose may sound perfectly
consonant at another time, depending upon what the ear becomes accustomed to.

In order to gain a fundamental vocabulary, we shall start with the more traditional
forms of triads (chords), cadences, and chord progressions. Then we shall proceed to harmonic material combined with flowing melodic lines tending toward the period style of
the romantic era. This style, it should be noted, is valuable for piano improvisation, for
it invites the rich possibilities of resonance producible by our modern piano. The nocturne,
boat song, waltz, and other freer forms are natural outcomes of this approach.

In the next chapter we shall study harmony as accompaniment, and thereafter take
up "quick tools" while experimenting in different period styles, including contemporary
idioms, followed by a search for essence—both being enlargements of the improviser's
harmonic sense.

EXERCISE 44 — Triads

Harmony begins with a chord containing three different tones and commonly called
a triad. A triad consists of a bass note with the interval of a third and a fifth above it,
and can be formed on each degree of the scale. Here are specific directions for use of the
triads.

Recite the names of the notes in each triad rapidly as you play them. This is *part* of the speedy, *automatic* process that will go on in your mind as you improvise, and it must be established at the beginning.

Key of C:

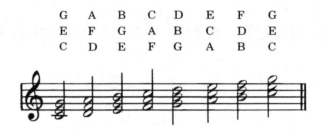

Write out the triads on each degree of the scale.

Transpose them to other keys.

With the eyes closed, visualize these, seeing their position on the staff. Although improvisation and sight-reading are not often related, it seems advisable occasionally to include the techniques for reading, especially through writing, thus strengthening the links between reading, writing, and improvising. The ear, eye, and finger faculties are thus united.

Then play with the eyes closed, left hand and right hand, to gain the feeling of the distances.

Here are the three positions of the triad on C. Try the triads on all degrees of the scale, three positions, in different ranges, high, low, etc., on the piano. Try gradations of dynamics (loud and soft, etc.) and listen to the differences.

Play all triads: major, minor, diminished (smaller than minor) and augmented (larger than major), see below.

Abbreviations:

    M = major

    m = minor

  Dim. = diminished

  Aug. = augmented

Try these in different registers. Compare them. You will find, for example, that the diminished triad has a very different effect from that of the major or the augmented or the minor.

Next, experiment with broken chords, using these triads, covering the whole range of the keyboard, crossing hands. Add pedal and listen to the effect. Change pedal with change of chord.

Example: C-major triad

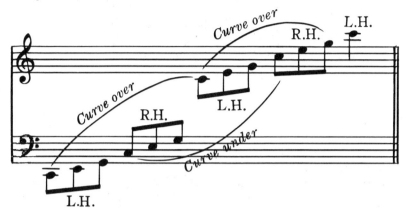

The technique for crossing hands: Start with the left hand (group CEG), and be ready to play the right hand an octave higher; while you play with the right hand, the left hand crosses over the right hand, describing a curve in order to be ready for the next left-hand group. When the left hand is over, playing that octave higher, the right hand curves underneath and is then ready to play the next group. There is a constant overlapping in curved motion.

EXERCISE 45 — Cadences, or Closing Harmonies

One of the best introductions to cadences comes through playing and listening to the great cadences found in Bach's organ works. I have introduced three of them here to be played on the piano.

Oddly enough, there seems to be more difficulty in recognizing cadences in two or three voices than in recognizing these full cadences. If at first you become well acquainted with these big chord cadences (especially by listening to the roots of the chords and then to the superstructures) and become sensitive to their logical and inspired successions of chords moving to a close, you will understand the principle of all cadences. Particularly when modulation (movement to related keys) is involved, you will then recognize those cadences in two or three voices more easily. Gradually your improvisations will include a wise choice of cadence. This tends to give shape to your improvisations, proper breathing spaces, and cadential feeling even while in motion. Here are examples of cadences from the organ Toccata and Fugue in D minor, by J. S. Bach.

$$V_2 \quad I_6 \quad I \quad V \quad V_7 \qquad I$$

$$I \qquad\qquad V \quad VI \qquad\qquad IV \ IV_6 \qquad I_6 \qquad V \qquad VI \ IV \quad I$$

Deceptive cadence   Final cadence

There are three functions of cadences:

1. *As Close:* in the sense of coming toward a finish, toward the ending of a composition, a section, or a phrase.

2. *As Progression:* logical succession of chords.
For example: there is an innate relationship between the tonic and dominant chords which exists whether this is expressed obviously or is subtly implied.

Starting with the tonic (I) and moving toward the dominant (V) the feeling is outward and onward ("half cadence"). Then that "dominant" feeling needs eventually to be resolved to the tonic chord ("authentic," or "perfect," "cadence").

When the subdominant chord (IV) moves to the tonic chord, you will recognize the "amen cadence"—also called the "plagal cadence."

The "deceptive cadence"—I, IV, V, VI—gives the feeling its name implies, that is, where you expect the tonic chord (I), and an end, you are given a VI chord; this is also called an "interrupted cadence," which keeps the feeling suspended.

Through working with cadences, you gain an understanding of a certain logical relationship of chords. Naturally, as you progress, you will be able to use these freely.

3. *As Modulation* (change of key): acting as a link from one section of a piece to the next. For example, in a composition in which the first section is in the key of C and the second section is in the dominant key (G), then, although the piece itself is in the

key of C, the cadence at the end of the first part moves into the key of G. One is then prepared to play that second section in the key of G. Often this transition occurs so smoothly that it is difficult to recognize.

Learn to play the following cadences. This is basic vocabulary. Memorize them first in C, then transpose and become able to play in all keys.

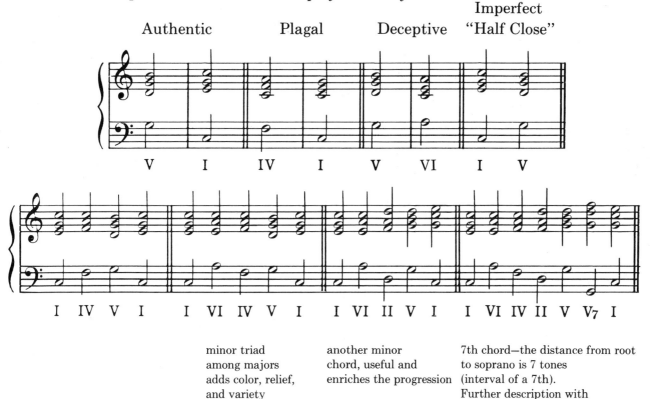

| minor triad among majors adds color, relief, and variety | another minor chord, useful and enriches the progression | 7th chord—the distance from root to soprano is 7 tones (interval of a 7th). Further description with cycle of 7th chords. |

EXERCISE 46 — Natural Progression of Chords

The generally accepted rule is to keep the common tone of adjacent chords in the same voice. This binds the chords together. At your musical discretion you will know when not to bind the chords and can then play them in freer positions in relation to each other. But at first keep the common tone in the same voice, as shown in the example below. The first inversion in the bass will also be useful for those whose experience already allows for it.

Notice that a descending 3rd, 5th and an ascending 2nd, 4th, and 6th in the bass form good progressions.

1. When you descend a 3rd in the bass, in the treble change one tone as you move from one chord to the next.

2. When you descend a 5th in the bass, in the treble change two tones as you move from one chord to the next.

3. When you ascend a 2nd in the bass, *all* tones move in the treble. The bass moves in contrary motion to upper voices.

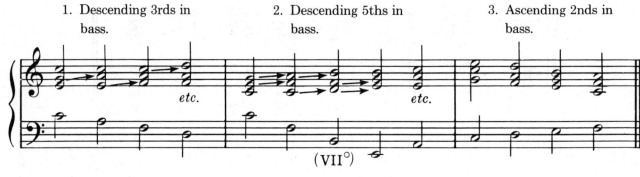

1. Descending 3rds in bass.

2. Descending 5ths in bass.

3. Ascending 2nds in bass.

Retain the two common tones, move the other tone up.

Retain the one common tone, move other two up.

No common tone. Move triads in opposite direction to bass.

In Example 2 (above) the diminished chord on the seventh degree of the scale can be altered to form a dominant chord.

Example of Progression: Descending by 3rds in bass chords.

Intermezzo, Opus 116, No. 6 (2nd part)   *Johannes Brahms*

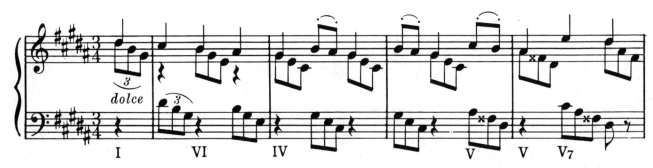

Combine descending 3rds and 5ths and ascending 4ths and 2nds in bass line. Example:

Further uses of the above: Try reverse movement in bass, that is, by ascending 3rd, ascending 5th, descending 4th, descending 2nd. What effect does this produce?

Try making all chords in the progression major, all minor, all diminished, all augmented. Then combine, finding the tone colors you prefer.

Examples:

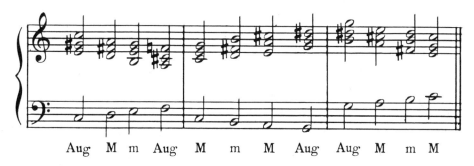

Aug   M   m   Aug   M   M   m   M   Aug   Aug   M   m   M

EXERCISE 47 — Character Changes of One Tone

First we shall study the character changes of one tone—how that one tone is influenced by various tones added above, below, and after it—and how the differences in sound affect the harmonies. This is directly for development of the ear, and for the ear in relation to the feeling.

Here follows an outline of the first part of the chord accompaniment of Schumann's *"Ich Grolle Nicht."* Listen to how the note C is sustained for seven measures. Notice the differences in sound as the changes take place surrounding C. Sing the C's while playing the chord outline.

Chord Outline

Ich grolle nicht

Robert Schumann

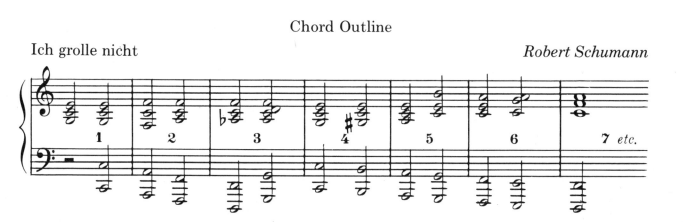

You will find that often a change of one note in a chord will act as an opening wedge, leading toward a climax of a phrase or a whole large section of a piece. At the same time, when you find one tone that acts as a sustaining thread (as the C in this example), a genuine sense of support is given to the whole musical structure.

Of course, the right choice of chord, arriving at the right moment of time in relation to the words of the song, is of primary importance and makes an interesting study.

EXERCISE 48 — Blending Harmony, Passagework, and Melody

Begin with the fundamental chords, I, IV, V, in the bass. As shown in the example below, in this exercise we are using open-position broken chords as contrasted to close-position broken chords, the latter known as the "Alberti bass," which was often used by the earlier composers. See the early Sonata in C Major, Mozart, for close-position broken chords, and compare them with the open-position broken chords in the example. Play the open-position chords below; listen to the resonance. You will find that these allow for a rich play of the overtones, in relation to the chord and the melody. Nineteenth-century composers were remarkably aware of the value of the open-position chords as accompaniment to their melodies.

Examples:

Combine broken chords in the left hand with the notes of the harmony in the right hand.

Examples:

EXERCISE 49 — Leaning Tones

Play a chord in the left hand and at the same time play an adjacent tone, *not* belonging to the chord, in the right hand. Feel the pull of that leaning tone—pulling toward a note of the harmony—and then resolve it.

Examples: Leaning tones in the upper part; ten possibilities are as follows:

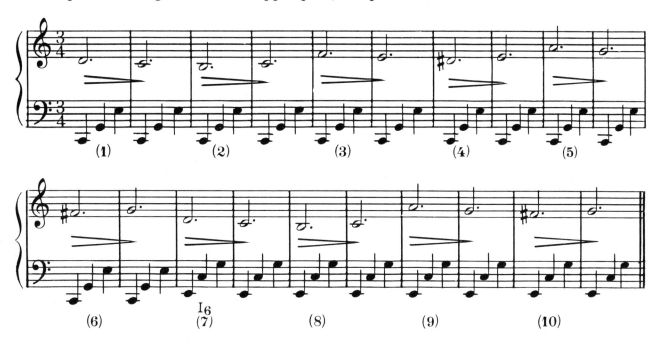

Note that with the inversion in the bass, you do not repeat the 3rd of the chord in the right hand. Too sweet!

Leaning tones and their movement to consonant tones give the sense of tension and relaxation. Dancers find these textures in music vital when they wish to express tension and relaxation either in their own dances or in their pupils' dances. When musicians playing for dancers can use these textures in their improvisation, the dancers are bound to feel and respond accordingly.

Examples: Leaning Tones in the Bass; fourteen possibilities are as follows (harmonic points are in the right hand)

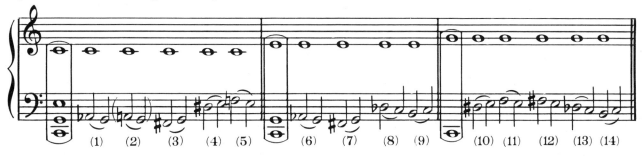

Hear this open C chord and sustain the sound of the C.

Write all leaning tones on all degrees of the scale. Consider leaning intervals as means of enriching the texture.

Listen to the differences in these sounds while you play each set. Give yourself a specific direction and confine yourself to one combination until you have felt and absorbed those sounds. To begin with, decide to play the broken chord on C in the left hand, with the leaning tones to C in the right hand. Do not allow anything else to divert you, regardless of how appealing another series may appear. This is part of the discipline of improvisation.

After you have absorbed each series and are thoroughly familiar with them all, then —*let go!* Let the sound provide the rhythmic patterns demanded. This might invite a nocturne, a boat song, a tango, or possibly a nameless, haunting melody with accompaniment. Later, when combining leaning tones with running, passagelike figures, you will be able to improvise quite desirable music in this vein.

The playing of masterworks has great value for the improviser, and you will find that, conversely, improvisation benefits your performance of masterworks, however simple or advanced. When you play a Chopin nocturne, for example, realize the nature of leaning tones and their resolution, as tension and relaxation. Through your own improvisations you will find that the whole emotional and physical response—your tone, dynamics, phrasing, and muscular and weight control—will integrate naturally and with true musical feeling.

EXERCISE 50 — Passagework in the Right Hand, Broken Chords in the Left Hand.

Directions: Combine broken chords in the left hand with flowing scalewise movement in the right hand. Again, the way to improvisation is through vigorous, strongly rhythmic work at first. Before producing more finished expression, one must often hew through rough-sounding material. This is a practical approach for the combining of passagework with broken chords. Given this impetus, you will find your musical ideas growing, and flowing melody as well as interesting design will emerge.

First try eighth notes in the right hand with broken chords in the left. Then triplets, then sixteenth notes, then varied rhythmic patterns.

Example: Triplet figure in the right hand, broken chords in the left hand.

Notice that three of the notes of the scale are consonant with the chord and four of the notes of the scale are not consonant with the chord. With the C chord the notes CEG are consonant and DFAB are not consonant. Observe that, when you play a tone in the right hand that sounds rough to you with the tone of the accompaniment in the left hand, the note adjacent to it will smooth it out. If only smooth sounds were expressed, they would become quite dull. The rough ones supply texture and beauty. Besides, to our contemporary ear none of these tones sounds particularly rough. As Leonard Feather has remarked in *The Book of Jazz:*

At this rapid tempo any series of fast-moving eighth notes is protected from conflict with the underlying chords.

The discipline here is to keep the scale line moving—first in eighth notes, then in triplets, then in sixteenth notes, scalewise, covering a distance of several octaves on the piano and gradually forming designs. Later include accidentals and different rhythmic patterns.

You will find that your harmonies in the bass will become more interesting as you include the minor chords in their relationship to the majors as shown above both in the cadences and in the natural progressions of chords. Review Exercise 46—Natural Progression of Chords.

In improvising with the above examples, sometimes the last few measures will act as a springboard and provide the impetus for continuing the improvisation. In the example in triplets (above), I later used different rhythmic patterns, and as a result, four measures grew out of the first measure of triplets, and the following measures extended toward a fairly interesting improvisation.

EXERCISE 51 — Characteristic Accompaniments in Left Hand with Broken Chords

Nocturne, G major   *Frédéric Chopin*

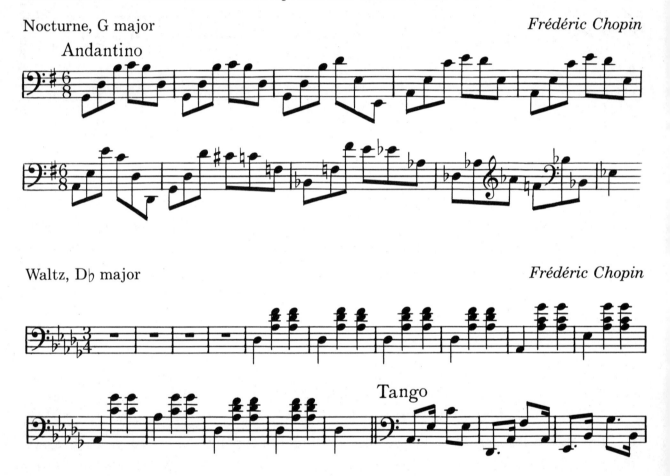

Waltz, D♭ major   *Frédéric Chopin*

For further examples see Felix Mendelssohn's *Songs Without Words*; "Venetian Boat Song"; see also *Tango*, by Isaac Albéniz.

Make your own examples and write them out. Try making melodies with this type of accompaniment. Go over the rhythmic patterns in Chapter III and choose some of them to use with the above patterns for accompaniment.

In conclusion, a few words on harmonic form. Taking the ABA form, here is an exemplification of the principle of harmonic form. The A part, a feeling of starting on the tonic and ending with a feeling of the tonic. The B part, starting on the dominant and ending on the dominant, providing a constant feeling of moving forward. The return to the A part has the tonic feeling.

Whether these basic feelings of tonic and dominant deal with simple question-and-answer, a song form, or sonata form, the same principle applies.

As a result of the rising tension toward the climax in the B section, so much energy may have been generated that you may not be ready to return directly to the A section. At the height of the climax a feeling somewhat in the nature of cadenza can be produced. (Here one can invent or execute some elaborately decorative passages.) It is almost as if you move higher than the climax and then you unwind. There is a gradual leading back toward A. This is particularly striking in the concerto. In the ABA form, the proportion of the rise to the fall is often three to one.

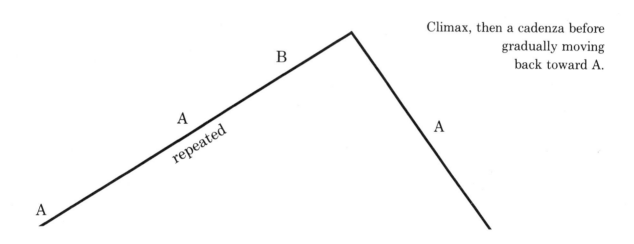

B

A
repeated

A

A

Climax, then a cadenza before gradually moving back toward A.

In contemporary music one may not easily recognize the actual chord expression of the relationship between these dominant and tonic feelings. The fundamental feelings are the same, however, whether actually expressed or simply implied.

CHAPTER XII

Harmony as Accompaniment

NOW WE shall advance to the improvisation of original melodies combined with accompaniments, thus enlarging upon your already acquired skill in improvising melodies and harmonies separately.

Some essential preliminary directions for accompaniments to melody are as follows:

1. Sing a familiar melody while tapping out the rhythm.
2. While playing the melody with the right hand, tap out with the left hand the rhythm you feel to be basic for the accompaniment.
3. Be consistent rhythmically.
4. One note, two notes, or a chord in the right place (on a strong beat—or an unexpected beat) can produce just the lift and support needed for your song, and your particular voice and type.
5. Avoid "thick" chords. (See the first version of the accompaniment for "Oh, Susanna!" and the remarks of the class, page 127.)
6. Try to anticipate the chord before you play it.
7. Consider the value of rests in accompaniment.
8. Listen from the bass *up* rather than from the top voice down.
9. Sometimes a good accompaniment is made with alternate movement between the accompaniment and the melody. See, for example, "O Waly Waly," arranged by Benjamin Britten, from his *Collection of Folk-Songs,* Vol. III.
10. Many songs have indications of chords—written above each measure—often with the guitar diagram. In popular music sometimes the chord indications are written above the melody (and people read only the melody and those chord indications). Sometimes it is taken for granted that the melody is known, and only the chords are indicated.

Leonard Feather, in *The Book of Jazz,* refers to this when he says:

The improvisational bases of jazz are not melodies, but chord structures . . . the uninitiated listener . . . must be instructed in following the new melody created by the jazzman, based not on the missing melody the listener is seeking, but on a harmonic routine identical with that of the unplayed tune.

Exercise 52 — Accompaniments to Songs

Make accompaniments to the following songs, using the chords found under "Cadences" (page 127) in Chapter XI.

1. Use two chords (I, V):
    Augustine
    London Bridge
    Three Blind Mice
    Hot Cross Buns

2. Use three chords (I, IV, V):
    Auld Lang Syne
    Believe Me If All Those Endearing Young Charms
    Coming Through the Rye
    First Noel
    I Saw Three Ships
    Begone Dull Care

3. Use the minor scale:
    Charlie Is My Darling
    A-hunting We Will Go

4. Use one modulation:
    Home on the Range
    Beautiful Dreamer
    I'm Called Little Buttercup (Gilbert and Sullivan)

During a class lesson with six young people, the subject of variety in accompaniment came up.

First the familiar tune "Oh, Susanna!" was chosen, and each person picked out the melody by ear, also transposed it in order to be perfectly familiar with the melody line.

Then each tried a different accompaniment and the other members of the group commented upon the results. It was found that the three basic chords, I, IV, V, were all that were needed to harmonize this tune (as is often the case with simple songs).

Then one girl tried the triads CEG, FAC, GBD in close position, the chosen triad on each strong beat as shown in the music below. The group decided that this version sounded "too thick" for the tune. Next, one student tried the same chords, close position, but in broken-chord form. "Better, but still somewhat heavy," the group decided. A boy who tried 5ths in the bass (while another played the tune) liked the results. One tried the second part of the tune in the left hand with the chords in the right hand. After some discussion and suggestions, another boy tried a descending line in the bass, single notes (with index finger). "It sounds like a twanging banjo," they said, "and it goes with the words."

The next, somewhat more technically advanced student tried the same idea but in broken octaves and commented that "the harmonies are implied." Later, several in the class played the transposed tune with chords, trying different rhythms, accents, rests, etc., in the bass, and then applied the same principle to other tunes.

This approach is fun, particularly for making accompaniments on the spur of the moment, and is open to all to enjoy.

Oh, Susanna!

This is a skillful example of motion music. Here, within the framework of an adaptable folk song, the accompaniment is so varied as to invite practically any dance movement that children (or grownups) would enjoy. It is clear, rhythmic, and uncluttered, an example of true simplicity and artistry.

Exercise 53 — Harmony as Accompaniment for Rhythmic Activity

1. Play the melody "Jim Along Josie," given below. 2. Pick out the melody by ear. 3. Play the chords in the bass (not broken). You will notice that the accompaniment uses only the I and IV chords. 4. Transpose the chords to the key of C by ear. 5. Break the chords as written. 6. Play the melody and the chords together.

After singing and playing the first, original version, you are ready for variations. The variations given below of "Jim Along Josie" are adapted to the various rhythmic activities of children while they sing. These include a walk, hop, run, jump, tiptoe, crawl, swing, roll, skip, and sit-down. The following roman numerals correspond to the song and numbered variations below.

"Jim Along Josie"—Song

A little fast, crisp

Hop jim a-long, jim a-long Jo-sie, Hop jim a-long, jim a-long Jo.

mf

As fast as possible, light

Run (jim) a-long, jim a-long Jo-sie, Run (jim) a-long, jim a-long Jo.

mp

Moderately fast, heavy

Jump jim a-long, jim a-long Jo-sie, Jump jim a-long, jim a-long Jo.

f

I. Sing and play the original tune in $\frac{2}{4}$ meter with accompaniment.

II. Notice change from $\frac{2}{4}$ to $\frac{4}{4}$ meter with a broken triad in the bass for the walk.

III. A slightly rough texture in the bass is made by including the interval of a 2nd (CD) superimposed upon the 5th in the bass. Besides giving the feeling of the hop, the 2nds CD and B♭C (second measure) give a percussive quality that adds bite.

IV. For the run, the melody is high in range, with the intervals of a 5th, a 4th, and a 6th in the accompaniment. An interval in the bass often gives much more lift and airiness than a whole chord, which might make it too thick for a light run.

V. For the jump, see the low bass, with 5ths, 4ths, and 6ths within the octave. This accompaniment gives impetus for the jump. The inner voice in the bass moves from C to B♭ and from C to D. The F in the bass acts as a drone bass, being evident throughout.

Moderate, quiet

Let's sit down now, jim-a-long Jo - sie, Let's sit down now, jim-a-long Jo.

VI. For "tiptoe along" horizontal intervals are used in contrast to the vertical intervals of IV. The F in the bass still rings out, though sounded only in alternate measures.

VII. This is "crawl along." Compare with VI. It is an octave lower with a sustained "organ point." The ties also help toward holding back the movement, which allows one to feel the nature of a crawl. Notice the end of the variation, which invites returning for the repeat of VII or continuing on to the next—VIII.

VIII. The big broken chords in the bass (open position) invite "swing along." This is the first change in rhythm to $\frac{3}{4}$ meter.

IX. For "Roll jim along" the rhythmic pattern is in sixteenth notes in the bass.

X. For the "skip," a clever choice of rests—"white space"—and rhythmic pattern has been made, with big broken chords in the left hand in high range.

XI. "Let's sit down." Compare with VI and VII. Listen for the low F sustained throughout. Feel the coming toward rest (sitting down). The suspended feeling at the end incites a desire to start all over again.

When making your own improvisations, remember these ways of varying a melody and accompaniment.

Examine your song literature from the point of view of the accompaniments. Examples: Schumann, Schubert, Hugo Wolf, Fauré.

Now we are coming to the next and exciting step forward for you. For the first time you will be combining (both) accompaniment and melody in your improvisations. Up to this point you have learned to harmonize a given melody. Now you will be able to improvise your own accompaniments while improvising your own melodies.

EXERCISE 54 — Simultaneous improvising of Accompaniments and Melody

1. Play one chord on the piano, for example, the C chord. Repeat the chord where or when the rhythm dictates it. Sing a scalewise melody in eighth notes with the chord accompaniment; then try different rhythmic patterns.

2. Play the three positions of any chord—quietly. Listen. Cover the keyboard with these three positions while singing a scale tune.

3. Play the C chord as given below. Sing the tones adjacent to C on the strong beat, that is, sing the tone on either side of C.

Feel the strong pull of the tone that does not belong to the chord but that gravitates toward it. This is an emotional pull—a rough sound moving to a consonant sound. Write out other combinations of leaning tones with basic harmonies. Cross hands as you play broken triads, and cover the keyboard while singing.

Here is a way to support a folk dance with a rugged accompaniment.

In the dance below observe that in Measures 1 and 2 the composer uses 5ths in the bass. He gives the swing of the dance by moving rhythmically down an octave and then up again to the next measure. In the following excerpt compare Measures 42 and 43 (numbered in example) with Measures 1 and 2.

In Measures 17 and 18, notice the clusters in the bass built on a triad with an added adjacent tone. The last chord is a D-minor chord with a G added.

The Irishman Dances*

Henry Cowell

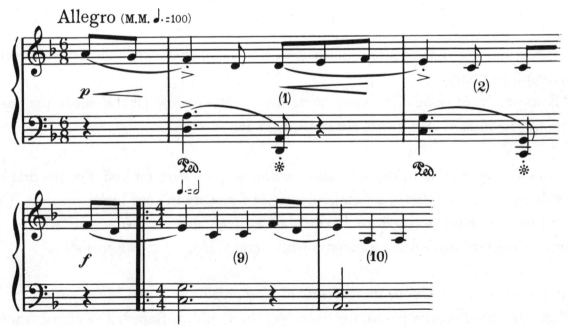

* Bars from "The Irishman Dances," by Henry Cowell. Copyright 1936 by Carl Fischer, Inc., N.Y. Reprinted by permission of the publisher. Appeared as an item in *Masters of Our Day,* educational series edited by Lazare Saminsky and Isadore Freed.

(Clusters)

In folk music and certain Oriental music in which a single line of melody for voice or instrument is complete in itself, and in which no accompaniment could possibly enhance the beauty of its expression, you should never attempt to add anything.

However, when you have a song that can be enhanced by good, vital accompaniment, there are many possibilities, including the use of 7th chords as being concord (consonant)—similar to Bartók's account of his use of accompaniment in Eastern European peasant music:

". . . the strange turnings of melodies in our eastern European peasant music showed us new ways of harmonization. For instance, the new chord of the seventh which we use as a concord may be traced back to the fact that in our folk melodies of a pentatonic character the seventh appears as an interval of equal importance with the third and the fifth. We so often heard these intervals as of equal value in the successions, that what was more natural than that we should try to make them sound of equal importance when used simultaneously. We sounded the four notes together in a setting which made us feel it not necessary to break them up. In other words: the four notes were made to form a concord." (From "The Influence of Peasant Music on Modern Music." by Béla Bartók, reprinted from *A Memorial Review,* pages 72 and 73, Boosey & Hawkes). Used here by permission of the publishers, Boosey and Hawkes.

(See the example from the Bartók *Rhapsody,* on page 138.)

CHAPTER XIII

Tools: for "On-Demand" Improvisation

MUSICIANS who are called on to improvise for dancers or other groups must have materials quite literally at their finger tips. They must think, so to speak, with their nimble fingers. They cannot afford to watch the keyboard, nor can they deliberately think of chord progressions, rhythmic patterns, and contrapuntal devices. They have time neither to speculate nor to contemplate the assignment. They need ready-to-hand tools to execute quick mental processes. For they must improvise music on demand; they must anticipate what they are going to need; they have to make good while in action.

Teachers, too, need materials they can put to quick use with their pupils or assign for homework. The aim is to make students acquainted with the whole keyboard and to gain facility and speed, while training in the whole field of musical improvisation is in progress. Demands upon the student's mind, emotions, and motor capability are made simultaneously.

The material presented here will provide exercises in quick mental processes and at the same time develop technical facility in improvisation. Our work here may be compared with the rapid processes of mental arithmetic, but of course one should never lose sense of the musical values involved.

EXERCISE 55 — Accompaniments in the Bass to Folk Songs and Improvised Melodies.

1. The use of 5ths (moving occasionally to 6ths) in the bass—almost like a drone bass.

Egyptian Melody

2. Implied harmonies by playing one note in the bass.

Wohin

Franz Schubert

See the original Schubert song "Wohin" and compare his evocative accompaniment with these implied harmonies in the bass.

Improvise original melodies with implied harmonies in the bass.

EXERCISE 56 — Quick Change of Key

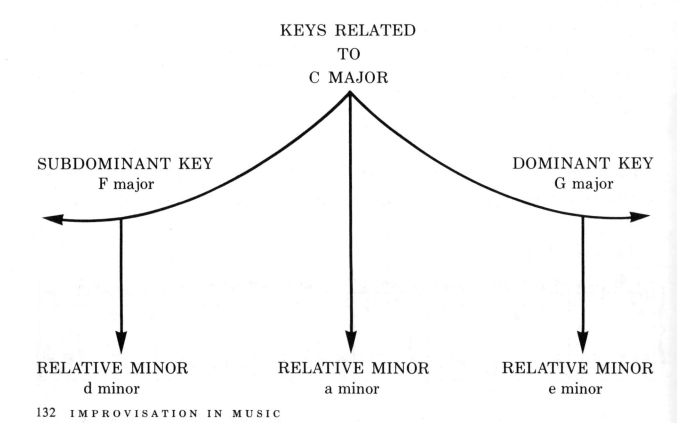

On the staff the related keys to C major are:

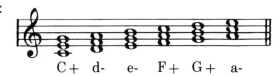

Preliminary drill: In the bass play the leading tone (seventh degree of the scale) then move to the tonic.

1. Play the seventh degree of the scale (with the fifth finger). While playing the dominant chord, first inversion, anticipate the next chord, resolving to the tonic.
2. Play scalewise passages in the right hand, repeating each set of V-I many times to ensure a real blending of scale passages with the chords in each key. In this way facility in the six related keys will be achieved, combining each scale with its basic chords. Later use complete cadences in each key.

After gaining facility with the keys related to C major, proceed to other keys.

EXERCISE 57 — 7th Chords as Texture, Moving from One 7th Chord to Other 7th Chords.

Say as you play:

"Retain three common tones, move one down."

"Retain two common tones, move two down."

"Retain one common tone, move three down."

A cadence can be produced with a dominant 7th chord and its resolution at any point. Combine with rhythmic patterns.

TOOLS: FOR "ON-DEMAND" IMPROVISATION 133

Imagine playing the game of Jerusalem! Six children march around five chairs. When the music stops, each child scrambles for a chair. One child is left without a chair. Then five children march and scramble for four chairs, and this game of elimination goes on until one child, the winner, remains. In using these 7th chords as given above, where would you stop to give the feeling of surprise and suspense?

Here is an example of descending 7ths in bass accompaniment. (Bartók, *For Children*, Vol. II, Rhapsody, #36–37, Measures 8 to 10. Published by Boosey and Hawkes.)

Here are eight types of 7th chords. Say and play:

M. triad	M. triad	m. triad	m. triad	Diminished triad	Dim. triad	Dim. triad	Augmented
+ Major 3rd	+ minor 3rd	+ M. 3rd	+ m. 3rd	+ Aug. 3rd	+ M. 3rd	+ m. 3rd	triad + m. 3rd

Play in different registers—left hand, right hand, crossing hands (using pedal); 7th chords can be used (1) as texture—moving from one 7th chord to other 7th chords, (2) for modulation.

With the eight types of 7th chords listed above, try progressions, retaining three common tones, two common tones, one common tone, as above. You will soon find favorite ones to add to your vocabulary.

Following your work with 7th chords, experiment with 9th chords. The general rule is: omit the 5th of the chord. Here are examples of 9th chords in sequence.

9th chords in sequence

EXERCISE 58 — Clusters

Add a note adjacent to one of the notes of a triad. This can be played as a cluster or broken.

EXERCISE 59 — Black Keys in the Right Hand and White Keys in the Left, and Reverse

Place your right hand directly over your left, the right hand on the black keys. Also try the reverse, black keys in the left and white keys in the right. With different rhythms these can make for gay, clever, humorous improvisations.

EXERCISE 60 — Simultaneous Use of Two Keys

In the example below, the key of E is in the right hand and the key of C is in the left hand. (This automatically forms all major thirds.) First play the scale of C in the left hand alone and then with the key of E in the right hand. Make an improvisation using both keys at the same time. One improvisation out of this grew into a sketch based on the characters of Pierrot, Pierrette, and Harlequin.

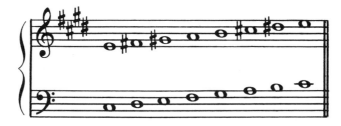

Try the keys of C and A major together, then C and F major together, and so on, each set giving different effects.

EXERCISE 61 — Harmonies Built out of Basic Intervals

Many of the experiences you gained in free counterpoint can now be utilized further. Play the intervals used in free counterpoint with the two thumbs. Example: C and E. Then open out into an octave with each hand, fifth finger on the upper E in the right hand and fifth finger on the lower C in the left hand. Then add one note in the middle of the octave in the right hand.

Write out a series as a framework, then cover the keyboard in a wide range.

Keep one chord in mind, add an adjacent note.

EXERCISE 62 — Finger Designs

Using three fingers, you can play six different patterns:

1 2 3,   3 2 1,   1 3 2,   3 1 2,   2 3 1,   2 1 3.

Using different designs, make sequences on the piano keeping to one set (for example, 3 1 2) for each sequence. Work up speed. Then with the thumb under, play: 1 2 3—thumb under, 1 2 3—thumb under, etc., making a scale passage. Now play: 2 3 1—second finger over, 2 3 1, etc., ascending, then descending. Cover the keyboard: (1) right hand; (2) left hand; (3) hands together, contrary motion.

BROKEN CHORDS

Here is a way of breaking the C-major triad in eighteen different ways.

Now work out the C-major triad open position in the left hand.

Here is an example of the broken chords in the left hand, with finger designs in the right.

Try accidentals in the right hand, then wider intervals in the right hand, then wider intervals in the left hand. The fingers are at your command. Don't let them run away with you. Try other sets of fingering. Examples: 2 3 4, 3 4 5, 1 2 4, 2 3 5, using three fingers. Then continue with sets of four fingers. Examples: 5 2 3 1, 5 4 1 2.

Allegro

Now play five-finger designs. Example: 5 4 2 3 1, letting the rhythm design ($\frac{5}{8}$ meter) be similar to the finger pattern, accenting with the fifth finger.

Next change to $\frac{6}{8}$ meter, in which case the accents arrive on a different finger each time (here on every seventh beat).

You will find many different designs as a result of this approach. These finger designs are good tools for speed, and for developing facility in piano technique. To do them, you must concentrate completely, remembering that the finger design and the tonal design must be maintained with strict control. This control is opposed to the mistaken notion of improvisation as idle wandering.

EXERCISE 63 — Numbers

Numbers have many uses in music—for fingering, for degrees of the scale, for numbering the measures. Roman numerals are used for chords; *8va* indicates an octave above, or below.

Here numbers will be used as degrees of the scale, and then improvisations will be made by taking any set of numbers, such as license-plate numbers, phone numbers, social security numbers, etc., can become a satirical play.

Example: 1 2 4307 (Auto license plate)

The meter and rhythm fall into place. In this example the rest, followed by the number 7, in Measure 2 seemed to give the theme a certain energy—it was propelled forward, and then a play on rests emerged. This melody came from an auto license.

Impressions can form the basis for on-the-spot improvisations and can be amusing for both the improviser and the audience. Let me give a personal example. A friend came to tea and was reminiscing about her visit to London. She and her husband, being detective-story fans, had visited many places, particularly bridges over the Thames, connected with the English detective stories they had read. She was also eager to see the Changing of the Guard at Buckingham Palace, and she wanted to be in London during a pea-soup fog. Ironically her wish about this fog was granted just when the Changing of the Guard she had come to see was to take place; she had the fog experience, but the guard was obscured.

That afternoon, while improvising at the piano, I made an improvisation using my friend's telephone number as melody notes for the theme, then the activities of her jaunt with her husband. Their peering down from bridges into the water to imagine detective-story corpses, the London fog, and the Changing of the Guard all became related. These impressions merged into an improvisation that my friend found quite amusing.

CHAPTER XIV

Search for the Essence

IN CONTRAST to gaining facility in music-making on the spot, there is the quest for the essential principles of the art of composition. Many of us feel a need for deeper probing and study, and our means must be slow, patient search in the music and ideas of the masters. The materials so compactly set forth in these works are most conducive to the development of our own musical logic. Through unhurried, contemplative work we shall find that our own harmonic sense becomes firmly established. We shall find that we are proceeding, not through imitation of the master composers, but through personal realization of their deep logic.

For those who want to engage in this slow search for the essence of composition, whether it be from a motive to improvise or from a wish to understand the masterworks and play them better, or to gratify the spirit of inquiry, this chapter contains procedure that has been tested for its value as the beginning of the search:

1. A chord outline of the Bach C-Major Prelude (from the *Well-Tempered Clavichord*, Book I) with directions for use.

2. Four versions of one Bach chorale for careful comparisons: The linear (horizontal) motion of the four voices produces the weaving of a texture that is firm, logical, and yet flowing. The slight changes in the linear motion in each version result in subtle changes of harmony.

3. Beethoven Prelude Opus 39, No. 2, entitled "Through All the Major Keys." A concentrated study in modulation, with Beethoven as teacher.

A good harmonic vocabulary is required for improvisation, with logical, discriminating choice of music progressions. After working with the material presented, the reader should continue to analyze music of different periods and types. You will observe that certain basic progressions obtain whether the music is categorized as pre-classic, classic, romantic, or contemporary, and whether they are hidden or obvious.

As you proceed, you will notice that many other elements enter into the scheme besides the actual change of chord. Range, dynamics, scalewise passages and broken-chord designs influence the shape and movement from one harmony to the next.

One chord may be spread over several measures, depending upon the idea and mood, rhythm and style of the piece. When a broken chord or scalewise passage is in action, however decorative in design, one must hear the complete, underlying chord, and not only a single note or two notes at a time.

You will probably find that you have a tendency to lag behind—in order to enjoy and listen to what has already been played. For improvisation, you must be ready to abandon the past sound and the sound you are playing at the moment; you must progress in thought and alert your ear to the approaching change of harmony.

Anticipating the next chord in your hearing while still including the play of dynamics and change of range, design and mood is part of the technique of improvisation. Before you change your chord, you have to hear the approaching move harmonically. Gradually, after a while, a whole series will come to be "in your ear" and at your finger tips.

EXERCISE 64 — Chord Anticipation

The Bach C-Major Prelude chord outline included here is an excellent study and preparation for this type of fore-listening and performance, as it maintains logical progression with broken chords.

After playing it through many times in chord outline form and becoming thoroughly familiar with it, play the first chord and while still holding it *anticipate* the sound of the next chord. Play the second chord and hear the third chord. Continue in this way through the whole outline.

Then play the broken chords as written, hearing the whole of the next chord (even though broken). Gradually several measures with several chord changes will be anticipated.

Compare with broken-chord designs in other Bach preludes. Later make your own chord outline and then break the chords, choosing various designs. Remain consistently with one design throughout, each time through.

EXERCISE 65 — Chord Outline of the Bach C-Major Prelude. Directions:

1. Learn the chord form first.
2. Using the Bach outline, play the same chord progressions but devise your own rhythm pattern and over-all design.
3. Then study the prelude as Bach wrote it. (Note: This is the Bach prelude that Gounod used as accompaniment in his "Ave Maria.")
4. Write out and analyze the chord outlines of several of the other Bach preludes, from the *Short Preludes and Fugues* and the *Well-Tempered Clavichord.*

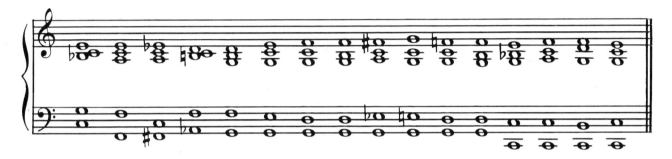

As written out by J. S. Bach

etc.

last 2 measures

How does this relate to improvisation? When you have experienced these compactly expressed harmonies, you will be in a state of mind conducive to musical logic, and this logic can act as a guide for your own expression, however simple at first your chord progression may be. If you work in this way, your sense of harmony and ideas for progressions will become established, not through imitation, but through realization.

EXERCISE 66 — Bach Chorale, Four Versions

In this section linear (horizontal) motion is compared with vertical structure. Bach often used the same hymn tune, making different harmonizations to meet the need of the particular cantata or Mass he was preparing. In the four versions of the chorale *"Christ lag in Todesbanden"* (two of them originally in the key of D minor, the other two transposed into the same key) the versions are placed one under the other so that each measure can be compared in all versions and the subtle differences recognized. These twelves measures in the four different versions offer many points of interest. The harmonies are produced as a result of the four individual horizontal lines, or voices, woven so as to blend. Through becoming aware of how each voice functions, you gain an understanding of how four individual lines moving horizontally produce true harmonies. Learn to listen to the change of harmony produced as the result of one different tone in an inner voice.

Directions (reading from left to right across the two pages):

1. Sing the hymn tune (the soprano) and play the bass line. Omit the other two voices.
2. Sing the hymn tune and play the alto (indicated by stems down in treble clef). Omit the other two voices.
3. Sing the hymn tune and play the tenor. Omit the other two voices.
4. Sing the alto and play the hymn tune with it.
5. Choose one voice (the soprano, alto, tenor, or bass) to sing, and play two voices.
6. Sing one voice and play the other three voices with it.

While pursuing this course, you will acquire a certain depth in music language and texture that might otherwise not be gained.

Record: Archive Production ARC 3063–14079 APM

EXERCISE 67 — Beethoven's "Through All the Major Keys"

There is a little-known prelude by Beethoven called "Through All the Major Keys," Opus 39, No. 2. The likelihood is that Beethoven composed it as a study for his pupils. Avoiding the more theoretic approach to modulation, we shall find this prelude a practical and inspiring example.

Beethoven begins in the key of C and modulates through all the major keys (not once but twice—the second time with usually only one measure in each key) with delightful variation, and then finishes with thirteen measures moving toward the key of C.

Directions: Count out and study the exact number of measures in each key. Play this work over many times, slowly, until you hear the changes of key and understand the values of the transitions. Through this focused listening, you will capture the sound within your *inner* ear. It will become so much a part of your basic vocabulary that later you will be able to translate these basic values into your own music terms *without* imitation.

For beginning your own modulation: Start with the key of C and move to the key of G (which is the dominant relationship). The first short cut in thinking is to ask yourself, "What is the basic difference between the key of C and the key of G besides the change of key tone?" Answer: F♯. Then introduce that F♯ harmonically in the bass:

and melodically by playing scalewise passages in the right hand. Commencing in the key of C, gradually change to the key of G by introducing the F♯ and resolving into the key of G. Construct a cadence to establish the new key firmly.

Go through all the keys in the same way. The signatures are all here in the Beethoven model.

Suppose your piece requires modulation through several keys rather than to a related key. You may then move gradually and smoothly—for example, from C through G through D to A—or, as a result of your particular rhythmic patterns, you may move rapidly through these related keys.

You may need to make a lengthy modulation from one key to a related key. Then, using Beethoven as a model (as when he has taken five measures to move from one key to another), try extending your own time form, similarly modulating slowly.

Then study the areas in which Beethoven modulates in one measure. That will teach you how to modulate rapidly. Notice his thirteen-measure finish after a deceptive cadence on A♭ and a coda.

Through All the Major Keys

Beethoven

With the music before you, choose the key changes you like best, and then begin to make your own variations on them. For example, instead of playing the chords in close form as Beethoven has them here, begin to break the chords. Then try different rhythms with the chords. Before moving on, maintain one chord for the length of time your particular rhythm needs to fulfill itself. Then make melodies (which may have grown out of your particular rhythm) and hear how this affects the modulation.

Change the range—to cover the keyboard. Here are expansive possibilities in sound. One needs to be able freely to cover the whole range of the keyboard by playing the same chord in different areas, and also one needs to be able to skip quickly from one range to another.

This prelude is most forceful; it generates tremendous action when used as a framework for improvisation. Playing this way, you might be reminded by free association of certain successions of chords that you yourself wish to move on to. Allow this wish to break through to consciousness and express the progressions your own inner ear is dictating. As a result of what Beethoven has expressed, this fresh impetus invites you to advance toward future experiments of your own.

In addition to its usefulness in the study of modulation, this prelude is also excellent for sight-reading. The signatures are clearly indicated, allowing for rapid, concentrated identification and performance in every key. One could go through any number of books of scales and chords over a long period of time and not gain as much as one can by reading and studying this prelude.

CHAPTER XV

Improvisation for the Dance

He who mingles music and gymnastics in the fairest proportions and best attempers them to the soul may be rightly called the true musician and harmonist in a far higher sense than the tuner of strings.   —PLATO

MUSIC for the dance can be simply an accompaniment, or it can be a deep, integral part of the dance. Qualities of movement can be expressed through rhythmic and melodic, harmonic and contrapuntal combinations of sound.

One form of music for the dance is the type the professional pianist catches and improvises while watching the rhythm, texture, and direct movements of the dancers. Later he composes, using these materials.

However, very often dance movement has implicit in it sound and rhythm that are not evident in the surface movement of the dance itself. The outer rhythm does not necessarily contain the inner rhythm that the dancer feels—the inevitable sound and rhythm that are unconsciously created in the substance of the dance. Unexpressed rhythms and sounds are going on, partly subconsciously, within the dancer, and should somehow be indicated in sound and rhythm to the musician, who can translate them into more formal settings.

Dancers familiar with the value of percussion accompaniment frequently use only the drum to indicate the rhythms and dynamics. More progressively, dancers can co-ordinate their own music with individual dances, or at least can hum or sing the melodies coursing through them while dancing. The tunes and counterrhythms may be vague at first. Nevertheless, original music by dancers does become definite as it is brought out and developed.

In directing a group, the dancer will find that the contrapuntal movements basic to music also are basic to the dance. When the laws underlying counterpoint are not merely understood theoretically, but experienced musically, the range of design and the structure for group dances are greatly extended.

Here is an example of music composed by a dancer who is experienced in music and improvisation. It includes cross-rhythms (counterrhythms)—with $\frac{4}{4}$ meter in the upper part, $\frac{3}{4}$ in the bass, and a more active $\frac{3}{4}$ pattern in the drum. The melody is based on an East Indian scale.

One of the richest experiences in group improvisation emerges when each person improvises with the voice while moving, while the others, too, are moving and singing, and when the ensemble "makes sense"—forms harmonies along with counterpoint.

EXERCISE 68 — Directions for Music Improvisation by the Dancer

Sing any one tone. Start with that tone while moving. Let the general pace and movement of the body dictate the sounds that follow. Imagine different settings (mountain or meadow, plain or shore) and move according to the mood that these evoke.

Turn and move in an opposite, or tangential, direction. Consider this change of direction as the beginning of a new music phrase.

For rests in the melodic line, allow for an occasional pause.

Now consider dynamics, expression marks, tempi, range, and contrasts.

> Scherzo – lively, quick-paced
>
> Andante – walk
>
> Maestoso – majestic, processional, heroic
>
> Adagio – feeling of resistance, of being pulled backward
> while moving slowly forward
>
> Fortissimo (*ff*) – contrast with pianissimo (*pp*)
>
> High range – contrast with low range

On the piano, start on C and move up a few notes scalewise, then down a few notes scalewise, forming a little design in sound, and finally land back on C (the present home tone). After experimenting with scale tunes on the piano, return to singing somewhat along the general scalewise line that you tried on the piano, but do not try to recall it note by note. It is the general idea, not the detail, that it is important to establish at this time.

Now you can begin to use different paces:

Walking (Andante). The musical term comes from the Italian *andare:* to walk. First walk around the room, setting a steady pace. Then stand at the piano, and while keeping that walking pace in feeling, make a scale tune, at an andante, or walking, tempo. Move away from the piano, andante tempo, and sing a scale tune. Do not try to recall the piano tune. Feel free enough to move and sing as the mood strikes you. Feel very quiet. You will soon hear your own melodies as you move, and be able to express them. In order to make scale tunes at other rates of speed, change your pace. Be sure to set your pace before starting to sing.

Running. Try a slow running pace. Sing a tune to that, not necessarily singing a note to each running step. Try to feel the mood of that run; then the tune will emerge. Sing a tone other than the home tone at the end of your phrase. Keep the tune unfinished. This will be somewhat like question-and-answer, described in the chapter on melody-making. Finish the final phrase on the home tone. Return to the piano, and with the tempo pulsing through you, try a scale tune with running notes. For the present, think of running notes as "eighth notes." As you may have slow runs or fast runs, try various tempi.

Skipping. Watch or imagine a child skipping. Clap the rhythm of a skip. Set your pace, keep it steady, move to the piano. With two fingers (thumb and index finger), make the fingers dance, approximately scalewise on the piano. Next, skip and improvise, singing as you move.

Hopping. Clap the rhythm of hopping, then imitate it on the keyboard. Listen to the sounds of the wide distances. Compare the low and the high sounds as well as the short lengths of sound.

Try staccato (short) *versus* legato (smooth, without breaks between tones). Now improvise a marchlike tune. When there is any question of pace, try marching or hopping or skipping or clap the rhythm. Then return to the piano and you will have the right rhythm for your melody.

Galloping. For this, first say: "And *ga*llop, and *ga*llop and *ga*llop." Next gallop and sing while moving. Imagine a horse galloping. With the second and third fingers try a galloping tune on the piano. You will soon find yourself making completely free melodies while improvising a new dance.

Thus far I have been speaking of improvisation by the dancer. Now let us adopt the musician's point of view. I can best illustrate this by an actual story of how a musician improvises music for a dance.

A dancer came to my studio one day and explained that she had an idea for a dance based on the movement of various machines in a factory.

She began to indicate the first movement. The heel and sole sounds on the floor, combined with her arm movements, carried out her original idea of factory and machine sounds. They called for contrapuntal rhythms, as well as percussive and dissonant qualities of sound on the piano. Appraising the individuality of this dancer, I knew that nothing very rough would be in keeping with either her or her potential audience. However, from my experience in improvising for other dancers with similar ideas, I knew that I had to have a certain amount of dissonance in the music texture. Roughness of texture in materials or in sounds invites highlights and also resolutions from the more dissonant to the more consonant effects. These are exciting and stimulating.

The difference between my dancer's metric accent on the first beat and her driving, more sparkling accent on the third beat suggested conflict between man and machine. This raced through my mind: texture—dissonance—accents—conflict.

Now the dancer began a second movement: $\frac{3}{4}$ meter, with the up-beat starting on the second half of the second beat. The relationships and contrasts between these various rhythms were already becoming apparent.

Next came the third phase of her dance. She said, "Somewhat like a windmill." While standing, she made wide circling movements with her arms, followed by a quick roll-over on the floor, then she rose with a rapid turning motion. Next she stood, and again indicated somewhat similar, wide circling movements by crossing her arms, making an overlapping—counterpoint. (Incidentally, I could not help wondering what a windmill movement would be doing in a factory. The dancer was from abroad . . . her English interwoven with German and French. She said something about "airplanes" and "wind.") She began to convey to me her sense of vastness.

I hastily jotted down as much of the rhythm and melody as I could. Ideas, musically, began to take shape. I could see, as I continued to watch the dancer, that the first theme would have to be steady, consistent, repetitive.

The first theme was stated—a translation of a machine movement, steady, almost monotonous, the accents giving it vitality and drive, a play between the two accents of different qualities.

The second part, after some repetitions, simply had to rise to a climax and become faster and faster, and the dancer responded eagerly to this idea. It was right, an inevitable movement arriving at a climax, the first excitement point.

At the third section, I began to see what she meant by "somewhat like a windmill." This vast circular movement, with a smaller whirr at the end, could be related to factory and machine, given the right music.

Here I had a little conflict with myself, from the viewpoint of the music. The theme needed to be stated in $\frac{6}{8}$ meter, and was somewhat lyric, and not so mechanical.

So I explained to her that "my improvising for this part seems to be moving toward the more lyrical."

The dancer liked the mood and theme of the music. It was the most melodic, so far.

Thinking it over that night, I thought it a good idea to let this third part of the music and dance symbolize the escape. Escape from the factory and machines, or from any mechanized behavior, into something quite lyric, seemed a good idea. I thought this theme might finally be the most important episode of the dance; that is, the episode having the most significant music and leading, in a later expression of it, to a genuine escape, not away from something, but into something higher—an escape *up*.

I could not resist calling the dancer early next morning to ask how she would like the idea of "the escape." She responded at once; she liked the idea. It was right ... psychologically and in every other way it was right to escape up and away from the dream.

I also explained that I would not mind introducing a lifting waltz rhythm as dream sequence the first time this section occurred, but that, in a later phase of the dance, the sentiment would have to be overcome, and a real work theme grow out of it.

After improvising that far, and going over the general idea and rhythms of the first three parts, watching the dancer as I played, a fourth part emerged. Thinking rapidly, I concluded that I should make this fourth section behave in the opposite way from Part 2. Part 2 rose in a crescendo and an accelerando. Part 4 would drop off, the speed would decrease (the left hand a staccato). The dancer suggested that as the speed decreased, I should lower the sound level (as a machine sounds when it slows down). Part 5 changed from waltz to genuine work theme—escape *up*.

We now had five movements—about half the length of the dance, the dancer said.

We realized that certain sections would have to be repeated. We also discussed entrance and exit. She would enter and exit with first-section material.

In building the music for her dance, I was aware that it could be a derivative of a rondo form.

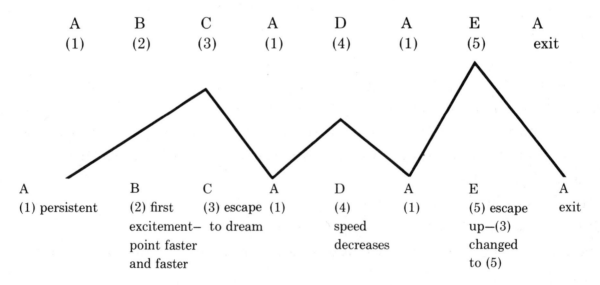

A	B	C	A	D	A	E	A
(1)	(2)	(3)	(1)	(4)	(1)	(5)	exit

A	B	C	A	D	A	E	A
(1) persistent	(2) first excitement— point faster and faster	(3) escape to dream	(1)	(4) speed decreases	(1)	(5) escape up—(3) changed to (5)	exit

Here we have had one experience with a dancer. Depending upon the creativity, the growing rapport, and the need, more subtle techniques can be used. The dance does not necessarily need to match the rhythm and movement of the music. Sometimes the music can appear in direct opposition to the dance, a contrapuntal play, producing tension that may or may not be resolved.

Another possibility enters, when a single chord (possibly spontaneously dictated by the dancer's movement) is followed by long silences, during which the dancer moves in her own rhythms; then another chord follows in musical logic. This can produce an inspiring relationship between dancer and musician.

For the dance I described above, it was convenient to improvise straight from short-hand notes, which indicated the rhythm patterns, themes, certain brief music figures, an occasional suggestion of bass accompaniment, chords, and lines suggesting contrapuntal motion, contrary motion, etc.

Sometimes at this point in extempore composition, we must decide whether to keep the work in an improvised state or begin to make a bridge toward a written composition.

If improvisation is decided upon, a record made on a tape is often sufficient. It is also possible to notate off the tape. Then one can keep the written piece exactly as improvised on the tape or alter the music after notating. An ideal arrangement is to find someone (preferably with perfect pitch) who will notate off the tape for you.

The process of written composition is certainly different—much more contained, studied, and framed. It is possible to maintain the sweep, the fluidity of the improvisational state and yet build and write good music for the dance. However, we must resist getting bogged down in the detail and avoid fussiness when writing. At the same time we must be ready to focus—to ponder, possibly to doubt, and to erase—while we are searching for the inevitable links, until a solution satisfactory to both the dancer and the musician is found.

The professional extempore composer needs to sharpen his musical tools by continuing to pursue every study available to him, including strict counterpoint, as, for the professional musician, there are no real short cuts.

For the young student, and for those possibly on their way toward professional careers, I know no more immediately rewarding and stimulating experience than music improvisation with the dance.

CHAPTER XVI

Rhythm Drawings and Pitch Pictures

I N WORKING with a group of small children, I have related music to drawing, and an account of how this was done may be instructive to the self-teaching improviser.

My aim was to help each child to find his own inner strength and individuality quietly, even though he was in a new group situation. The approach was intended to assist him to become free for true music activity. One approach that has proved very successful for this purpose is the making of rhythm drawings and pitch pictures.

For part of each lesson the children were seated, each at his own table, and given large sheets of blank newsprint paper and good crayons of various colors.

I clapped certain combination of long note and short note patterns while the children listened and then clapped them with me. For example, I said, "Clap these with me!—long, short, short—long, short, short—and long, long—short, short short short." Then the children chose their own long and short note patterns and clapped them.

Then I said, "When I begin to play long and short notes on the piano, you begin to draw. As you listen, draw long lines for long notes, and short lines for running notes in time with the music."

Their rhythm pictures soon showed free, sweeping curves or sharp lines and various shapes.

"This Old Man" is a rhythm picture made by a girl during her fifth lesson. She had been playing a simple version of the English folk song "This Old Man" on the piano, and she needed to feel a sense of continuity, as she was halting at the ends of measures. She made these rhythmic patterns while we both sang the melody. She suggested the arrows to indicate the direction of the lines, and drew the picture of the old man with the dog and the bone, within the accented final curve.

Her playing became rhythmic, with an easy continuous flow, gained partly through the experience.

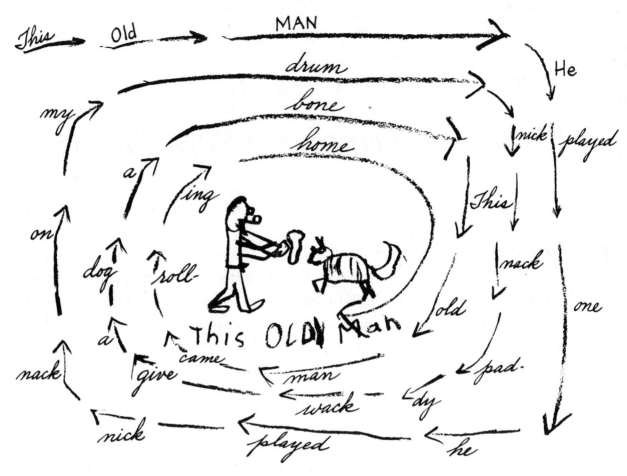

In "This Old Man," a folk song used in the film *The Inn of the Sixth Happiness,* follow him around, via the arrows. This is his rhythm pattern:

Now make a pattern of your own, while singing this same song.

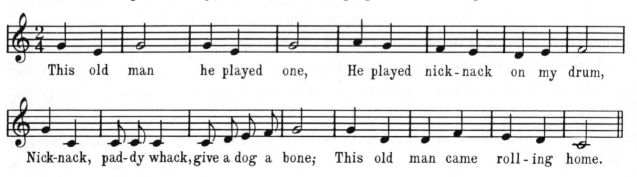

This old man he played one, He played nick-nack on my drum,

Nick-nack, pad-dy whack, give a dog a bone; This old man came roll-ing home.

In the young children's class we proceeded to pitch pictures.

I played notes in high range on the piano, then low range, and sang a generally ascending melodic line, then a generally descending melodic line. The children listened and made line drawings as I played. They noticed that some sounds were louder and some softer, making heavier and lighter lines; some brighter tunes sent them to the more vivid colors, some sounds led them to choose different colors in their pictures.

This is the way a pitch picture looks of the first part of "Home on the Range"

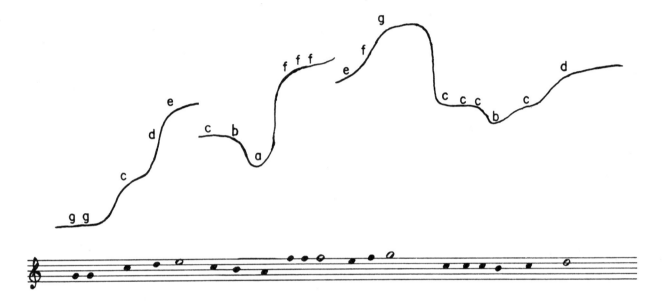

I then played the "Cache-cache" (Hide-and-Seek), from the Mozart *Les Petits riens,* which has a nice feeling of echo in the repeat of each phrase, and as a climax it has the "surprise" ending. We repeated the making of rhythm drawings and pitch pictures, and often gained fresh music experiences. The children's line drawings became an excellent by-product. Through the rhythm drawings and pitch pictures the class became individually and collectively aware and ready for rewarding music experience. The drawing was a means toward awakening a live musical response.

"Cache-cache," *Les Petits riens* — Wolfgang Amadeus Mozart

The opposite of listening to music while drawing is, of course, to start with your own line drawing, and let that induce the music improvisation.

Try drawing lines freely in curves, in angles—with plenty of white space around them —and try singing as you draw.

Out of this practice can grow interesting melodic lines, including ornamentation of an original melody, and a rising and falling melodic line moving to climactic heights and then to resolution.

It is also stimulating to start with a painting and to improvise music with it.

For the opening program of a nonobjective art exhibition (from the Guggenheim Collections) in Washington, D.C., I was asked to make music improvisations to some of the paintings. Just as one can watch a dancer and translate her movement into sound in a music improvisation, so too one can feel in certain paintings the sense of musical movement. I found the Wassily Kandinskys and the Rudolf Bauers at the exhibition particularly inspiring. A young pupil of mine who was at the exhibition picked up the idea and later followed through with music improvisations of her own to paintings, as well as to her own drawings.

What happens when I relate music to painting?

While I view the picture, I listen for the theme that is emerging from within myself. I find that the form, along with the lines, curves, and color, invites the movement, texture, and development of the music improvisation.

At another time, while I was studying a reproduction of the Rudolf Bauer painting *Three Points,* the contrapuntal form of the design came to me immediately and I began to play with contrapuntal tensions through what is called reflection, contrary, or opposite motion, as the lines seemed to demand. I quickly observed that the pattern of the picture ran in threes.

The tone colors made me think orchestrally, and I soon wished that I had three or four extra hands to be able to indicate on the piano in sound and rhythm the color and excitement of this painting. The colors moved from pink shades toward deeper reds, with counterpoint of blue bars and an odd touch of yellow that made for unexpected contrasts to the sharp angular blacks and the green background.

As I kept improvising and observing this picture, the music became more and more like a dance. Then I became aware of what seemed to me to be the resolution of the whole piece in the design in soft greens in the lower right. A critic said to me, "The part you composed for the green gave a feeling of consonance as contrasted with the other music, which had sharpness and a certain tense dissonance."

For myself I have experienced the truth of Herbert Read's remarks on Kandinsky:

A composition thus becomes an orchestration of vital forces expressed in plastic symbols. The music analogy is always in the background, and the concepts of time, rhythm, interval and metre hitherto reserved to music are freely introduced into the aesthetics of painting.

CHAPTER XVII

Group Improvisation

ERNST T. FERAND has noted that today "many more opportunities lie open to music instructors, beyond the education of professional musicians, in the sphere of laymen's education, in the school and even in the kintergarten." Dr. Ferand was concerned, as this book has been, with the problem of a creative music education: the bridging of the gap between active music-making and passive listening. "This can be achieved," he argues, "by abandoning music education based exclusively on interpretation, on mechanical drill and imitation or on abstract theory." We must give more attention to the improvisatory element, for "allowing more play for the individual to create and invent would bring theory and practice closer together, and would win over to a more enduring, livelier music activity (as amateurs) many children and adolescents who are repelled by the monotony of technical and theoretical instruction."

In this chapter I propose to go into the kindergarten, the school, the lay adult group, and even the music-teacher group to show how we give more attention to the improvisatory element. I shall give a number of illustrations of "more play for the individual to create and invent."

First, let's go to kindergarten and see a basic preparation being made for spontaneous yet disciplined improvisation.

Imagine six or eight children with percussion instruments, seated in a semicircle around the piano. One child, using a pencil for a baton, stands up and conducts. Each will have a turn being conductor. At first each conductor learns how to beat $\frac{2}{4}$ $\frac{3}{4}$ $\frac{4}{4}$ meters while I improvise and also play folk tunes, dances, and short pieces composed especially for children by the master musicians. This is the more usual use of the percussion band. The children follow with their drums, triangles, castanets, tambourines. Soon each child conductor is able to choose and set his own tempo and indicate his dynamics to the group. He learns to show them when to play fortissimo and pianissimo, crescendo and diminuendo, presto and lento, and particulaly when and how to start and how to stop. While responding to the conductor's vigorous beat, the children make various rhythmic patterns of their own, including eighth notes, dotted notes, and rests at certain points. This is the beginning of improvisation.

Sometimes I pick up the young conductor's beat at the piano, giving him the sense of command. At other times I lead at the piano, in order to introduce a fresh suggestion, because the children sometimes get into a groove and repeat the same pattern again and again. (Yet there are occasions when it is valuable for children to repeat certain patterns that have meaning for them at the time.)

After the conducting, they sing folk songs and move around the room. Each child in turn is leader and sets the pace—walking, running, hopping, skipping, and so on. At first I improvise as they move. Then they improvise melodies, singing as they move.

This might appear to be a usual music experience for children of kindergarten age, but it is not, as we have in mind the basic preparation for spontaneous yet disciplined improvisation. For example, an early form of self-discipline consists in learning to start and stop on the proper beat. *Before* one begins to play, one must be ready to start by establishing the basic rhythmic impulse and by listening for an inner melody. Finally, the improviser must be his own conductor and performer and must know exactly when to start and when to finish. This prevents wandering.

Now let's look at a group of eight-year-olds who are seated around a table with their autoharps and xylophones, recorders and drums. They are ready to begin. It is important, by the way, that children's instruments be of good quality—not toys.

Besides improvising melodies, these children are learning to play rounds (including "Three Blind Mice," "Frère Jacques," "Row, Row, Row Your Boat") with recorders and xylophones. This experience introduces a flavor of the beginning of counterpoint, which is followed by elementary work in progressions of intervals and in alternate movement in two voices. As a result, they are able to reach a musical level on which group improvisation can be adroitly introduced. They also realize that certain tunes make good rounds, whereas other tunes are better either left completely alone or played with chord accompaniment on their autoharps (and later piano). Autoharps are useful up to a point, but having the children remain with the basic I, IV, V chords for too long might produce a certain stagnation. Many are likely to feel that those are the only chords that exist for accompaniment; more varied combinations are introduced a little later on the piano.

One boy in this group is especially free with the autoharp, and he accompanies the folk songs easily. While he plays, other children improvise their own melodies, by singing and by using their own xylophones and recorders. Here they get a taste of combining melody with harmony.

Some of the children move over to the piano and learn to play simple accompaniments in the bass, discovering chords that fit the pitch of their tunes. This naturally leads to simple transposition.

Now let's come to a group of grownups who, as lay musicians, as parents or teachers, would like to practice improvisation.

"How do you start this group improvisation?" one asks.

I begin: "Suppose all of you clap the simplest, most basic, pattern in rhythm—$\frac{2}{4}$ meter, just two beats in a measure. Feel a strong impulse on the first beat and let the second beat rebound out of the strong beat. This is like a bouncing ball. You do not need to bring the ball up—it comes up by itself."

Let us assume that there are thirty or forty in this group. All begin clapping—first in $\frac{2}{4}$ then $\frac{3}{4}$ $\frac{4}{4}$ and $\frac{6}{8}$ meters while I conduct. Some are soon clapping eighth notes, triplets, and other patterns.

At this point, I explain the question-and-answer approach, outlined earlier.

The reader will remember that I said to children, "When we have conversations, and someone asks a question, where is the voice at the end of the question?"

The children generally answer, "Up."

"And when you answer the question, where does your voice land?"

"Oh, it lands down."

"Now I'll ask a kind of question in music sounds, and you see if you can answer it in music sounds."

In order that the rhythm may remain unbroken, it is important to respond immediately. Because, in music, one is filling up a time-space with rhythmic patterns, sound, and dynamics, the pulsation cannot be stopped and broken into by hesitation. We want no holes in the time-space.

I sing a music phrase, leaving the melody suspended, anticipating an answer. Sometimes the pupil just waits—nothing happens. If he does not respond, or if uncertainty appears, we return to the rhythm alone. I "ask a question" on the drum, or I clap it, so that he can answer that rhythm. If he still hesitates, I sometimes say, "You know, music-making is something like diving. Before you dive, you stand on the springboard and look at the water and wish that you could dive in, but nothing happens. Then suddenly you decide to plunge, and there you go. Now let's try the same idea on the drum. I'll start, and you just dive in and answer."

Then we continue with the melody-making, and, curiously enough, these spontaneous melodies are usually very good. Now this response is important, psychologically, for the growing child and for adults, too.

Soon there are many questions-and-answers, motives and bits of melody coming from all sides, all different, yet all blending in a good first group improvisation. The rhythm, scale, and key are the foundation.

At a music school settlement, a group of young teachers met with me in the auditorium once or twice a week. After a long day of teaching music to children, they were eager to gain a fresh impulse for their own music through improvisation.

In this auditorium were two "Greek" pillars, several steps, and some old red hangings. These, our properties, became in turn a Greek temple, a village green, a wide open plain—many different settings as the mood, rhythm, or chosen scale demanded.

Here was a group most eager to improvise, to gain experience, to experiment toward teachable results in improvisation. At the time, I was keenly interested in the use of unusual scales, but before this group could experiment with these unusual ones we had to begin with the more familiar scales, somewhat as follows: we discussed, chose, and then prepared the meter, pace, and rhythm, the dynamics, scale, and general plan of chords, the approximate position of the climax, and movement.

After the scale was thoroughly established and each teacher had had a turn at improvising, singing a free melody around the scale as a basis, the chords with more involved cadences were added. Sometimes one would clap the rhythm while several others beat drums, another student played the chords in whole notes, and the others improvised free melodies with more and more interesting designs. Two young women played the violin, and that instrument lent its quality as well.

Then followed the modes—the Aeolian, the Dorian—preferably sung without piano. Deeper levels were reached, using the voice alone, at first. Then no outside instrument could intrude or act as a barrier.

With rapport well established and imagination released, often a fine improvisation would grow, with a texture in sound and harmony, rhythm and movement surprising to this young group of musicians. Sometimes with eight people working at once, there would be a complete feeling of unity and inspiration.

EXERCISE 68—Group Improvisation, Including Syncopation—Directions:

Sing notes in the bass to rhythm.

First tap out 1) alone, then add 2), then 3), then 4), then 5). You will find that more and more vigor and excitement come into play.

Next, compose your own set of rhythms, starting with the shortest even note value, as for example in 1).

After this warm-up, in our exercise, formal directions are abandoned and a free group improvisation comes into play.

Each participant must listen intently to his own melody and at the same time be alert to the others' improvising. One expresses a theme or fragment inviting enough to be picked up by another member and carried on, possibly extended or caught up by still another; sometimes two make a contrapuntal play of it, while the others move along at a steadier pace. Rests enter where silent space is needed. While the harmonies and rhythm are continuing, all weave their way into a consistent texture. It is like a stimulating conversation in which one, then another, catches the idea, the theme, plays with it and passes it on, or invites a response, so that the idea is played upon with variations, and development follows.

I have witnessed this process in flamenco dancing in Madrid. The performers (about fifteen) were seated in a semicircle. An older woman started clapping, setting the pace. Then another started clapping off the beat—syncopated. Gradually more and more of them joined the clapping. Then either the guitarist or a man or woman solo dancer or singer performed to the background of the clapping, until they worked up to a peak of intensity and excitement.

When dancers who have had music training and acquired the ability to function fairly easily in both music and dance work with musicians who in turn have had some dance training, impressive results are achieved. Six-week intensive courses in the summer often give the best results when the teaching schedules are not too crowded. When the dancers are ready for music training and musicians are ready for the dance, a genuine blend of the two arts will arise from their joint professional backgrounds. Let me describe one such course.

The musicians had daily sessions in the early morning. They worked on advanced music improvisation—both contrapuntal and lyric materials—and also studied masterworks. Then the dancers and musicians joined in rhythms and body-limbering. This was followed by a session for the dancers alone in music improvisation and music literature for the dance. In the evening hours the two groups met and worked together, exploring and finding a common language.

Improvisations were made by the musicians while watching the dance movements. The musicians learned to be so free that they scarcely needed to look at the keyboard; they could feel for the notes while hearing the chords, melodies, counterpoint—this, while watching the dancers. (Incidentally, we built up this technique in the morning classes sometimes by having the musicians play with eyes closed or by looking away from the piano while imagining a group of dancers.)

The musician at the piano watched the dancers and the direction on the dance floor. When a dancer was ready to turn at a phrase, the musician ended his phrase, and moved on to the next. When other dancers entered, counterpoint often took over. Here was a counterplay between the dancer and musician. The form of both music and dance became quite clear, as well.

It was not at all incongruous or dissonant. A unified and harmonious expression often happened. One received a sense of a whole group working together, saying without words what only music and movement can state.

Sometimes the students changed places: the dancers took turns at the piano and the musicians moved out on the dance floor. If the dancer did not feel quite free enough to go to the piano, she would sing or whistle or indicate her music feeling in some other way. The musician then picked up the theme, or snatches of her melody, repeating, enlarging, continuing it. Hearing the sounds from different parts of the room while the dancers were moving created impressions that made for new developments. When the musicians did not feel quite free about their dance, they, with a movement of the arm, or at least with general movements, found that they could indicate what they felt, to catch the idea.

In this way the musician was no longer bound by the sense of form that he had been taught as the framework for music composition. Until music is approached in relation to the dance (or drawing or dramatic play, etc.), the musician remains within framed music form. But as soon as he improvises, watching dancers or moving as for a dance, something happens uniquely to the whole shape of the music.

The dancer, too, has been influenced by the traditional forms of the dance. However, when she hears music that has not grown out of specific dance forms or already composed music, something different and genuine is stirred up in her too. When interplay between the musician and the dancer grows, and when dancer and musician arrive at the ideal state in which each becomes both dancer and musician within himself, then very stimulating improvisation occurs.

CHAPTER XVIII

A Model Improvisation

AS EXPLAINED at the outset, the essential elements in building an improvisation are harmony, rhythm, melody, form, counterpoint, imagination, and these should finally make one cohesive whole. Let us now construct an example in which all these essential elements enter.

We can make an excellent start with the "amen cadence," since most people are familiar with its sound and associate it with two simple basic harmonies. The "amen cadence" is built on the IV chord (subdominant) followed by the I chord (tonic).

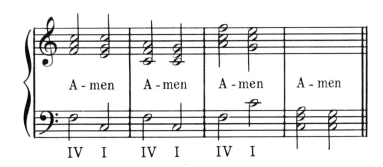

Sing the bass and listen for the root of each chord. The root is similar to the foundation of a building. The foundation should be laid first. The top line (*i.e.,* the soprano) is like the roof of a building. You might see it (hear it) first, but without the consciousness of the foundation (the bass) it is incomplete.

The element of imagination is essential, for without true imagination our experiment may become simply an uninspired expression. Act on the suggestions in Chapter VI for "sparking" the imagination.

Related to the mood of the "amen cadence" are many of the Psalms. For the purpose of building a model improvisation, I recommend the Twenty-fourth Psalm because of its eloquent question-and-answer pattern.

1. The earth is the Lord's and the fulness thereof; the world, and they that dwell therein.
2. For he hath founded it upon the seas, and established it upon the floods.

3. Who shall ascend into the hill of the Lord? or who shall stand in his holy place?

4. He that hath clean hands, and a pure heart; who hath not lifted up his soul unto vanity, nor sworn deceitfully.

5. He shall receive the blessing from the Lord, and righteousness from the God of his salvation.

6. This is the generation of them that seek him, that seek thy face, O Jacob. Selah.

7. Lift up your heads, O ye gates: and be ye lift up, ye everlasting doors; and the King of glory shall come in.

8. Who is this King of glory? The Lord strong and mighty, the Lord mighty in battle.

9. Lift up your heads, O ye gates; even lift them up, ye everlasting doors; and the King of glory shall come in.

10. Who is this King of glory? The Lord of hosts, he is the King of glory.

Chart out of the whole Psalm

1. Statement
2. Cause
3. Two questions
4. Answer (plus 5)
6. First conclusion
7. Command: "Lift up your heads . . ."
8. Question: "Who is this king . . . ?"
9. Command: like 7
10. Question: like 8. Answer: "The Lord of hosts . . ."

In setting a poem to music it is necessary to make the rhythmic inflections very strong in order to be able to produce a true melodic line.

Repeat the words with understanding, exaggerating the rhythm patterns. Observe the accented places. Tap out or move to the rhythm of the words, somewhat as a conductor would move to indicate to the choir the sweep, rhythm, and direction of the lines.

Draw a general line design on paper or in the air of the rhythmic patterns as you see them. Long lines for longer time values, short lines for shorter time values.

Here is one possible rhythm pattern.

The earth is the Lord's and the ful-ness thereof.

Now to sing the Twenty-fourth Psalm. Feel the melodic quality of the words. Let it be a "free" improvisation!

Here are the steps to be taken:

Say the words first.

Intone the words; murmur this Psalm quietly, almost to yourself.

Find the accented places. Gently tap out, or clap, or indicate in some way the accented places.

Draw on paper, or in space the general line or curve the words might take as a melodic line.

Hum or sing the first verse. Does it feel somewhat suspended? Like a question? Or does it feel like a complete statement? Notice the two questions in the third verse. Are they on the same level?

Continue through to the end of the Psalm. Do not criticize or halt, but move on without holes in the time span. You understand that rests within the rhythm of the piece are desirable, but halting or hesitation impedes the flow of improvisation.

For the sake of form, draw the long, sweeping lines of each phrase, first, freely, without actually indicating the words, through half-saying, half-humming the words to yourself. Then sing the words of the whole Psalm, cover the whole page with phrase curves until you find the general pattern consonant with your musical perception.

Each individual's feeling, mood, cadence will be different, resulting in a different form-as-a-whole in each case.

Next you might like to experiment with two-line drawings (or two voices) growing out of your experiences in free counterpoint.

Returning to the "amen cadence," now in two voices, notice how the F leans toward the E and is supported by the sustaining C below it. (A "leaning note" is sometimes called an *appoggiatura,* from the Italian *appoggiare:* to lean or support.) You will hear the interval of a fourth move naturally to the interval of the third.

Listen to the F move to the E while the C remains stationary. Listen, and feel the pull of the interval of a 4th to a 3rd, and of a 5th to a 6th. (In certain cases, the 5th pulls to a 6th. Sometimes the 5th stands on its own and you do not feel the same pull.)

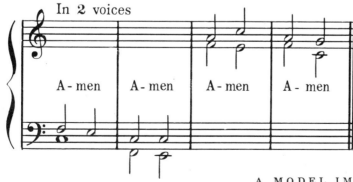

For other "leaning" relationships and other contrapuntal devices, refer back to Chapter X. In that chapter we used graphs to illustrate all the two-part work. Here we advise drawing with two free lines, similar to the rhythm and pitch pictures made in the manner shown in Chapter XV.

The above directions must be synthesized and rapidly co-ordinated both in your feelings and in your music. Retain the general feeling of the "amen cadence" underlying the whole improvisation, for its associations usually evoke an exalted mood.

By way of recapitulation:

Choose a favorite Psalm or poem, picture or idea. Blend the following elements:

Rhythm: Tap out the rhythm that seems right to you.

Melody: Chant, improvise a simple melody, being aware of the rise and fall of the pitch.

Harmony: Listen and play various cadences, including other chords within the mood.

Counterpoint: Gain the sense of tension and relaxation of one tone to another in their underlying interval relationship. Add other contrapuntal devices when your idea demands it.

Form: Chart a whole Psalm, or poem, as above. Draw a general pattern with phrase curves. Experiment with many combinations for structure.

Imagination: Invoke the exact feeling associated with your basic idea.

Relate these in one swift synthesis. This is what can happen in an improvisation.

CHAPTER XIX

A Little Anthology for the Improviser

Whistling Dick:

As Whistling Dick picked his way where night still lingered among the big, reeking, musty warehouses, he gave way to the habit that had won for him his title. Subdued, yet clear, with each note as true and liquid as a bobolink's, his whistle tinkled about the dim, cold mountains of brick, like drops of rain falling into a hidden pool. He followed an air, but it swam mistily into a swirling current of improvisation. You could cull out the trill of mountain brooks, the staccato of green rushes shivering above chilly lagoons, the pipe of sleepy birds. "Whistling Dick's Christmas Stocking" by O. HENRY.

Style, (like good manners) should never be self-conscious, but must express a free improvisation in a way that laborious application can never achieve. ALAIN

Extempore playing is very rapid composition in which a player imagines music and then plays it by ear . . . but the proportion able to extemporize even a definite march or minuet or anything that is clear-cut in form seems small.

Attributed to SIR JAMES SWINBURNE, F.R.S.
Oxford Companion to Music

HANDEL:

. . . he wrote as one speaks, he composed as one breathes. He never sketched out on paper in order to prepare his definite work. He wrote straight off as he improvised, and in truth he seems to have been the greatest improvisor that ever was. He wrote his music with such impetuosity of feeling and such a wealth of ideas that his hand was constantly lagging behind his thoughts, and in order to keep apace with them at all he had to note them down in an abbreviated manner. But (and this seems contradictory) he had at the same time an exquisite sense of form. *Essays on Music*, by ROMAIN ROLLAND

BACH:

Forkel says:

Bach, when improvising, usually confined himself to a single theme. Often he treated a theme for hours.

Bach's *Musical Offering* was first an improvisation on a theme given him by Frederick the Great, which he later composed and dedicated to the king.

DEDICATION

Most Gracious King!

In deepest humility I dedicate herewith to Your Majesty a musical offering, the noblest part of which derives from Your Majesty's Own August Hand. With awesome pleasure I still remember the very special Royal Grace when, some time ago, during my visit in Potsdam, Your Majesty's Self deigned to play to me a theme for a fugue upon the clavier, and at the same time charged me most graciously to carry it out in Your Majesty's Most August Presence. To obey Your Majesty's command was my most humble duty. I noticed very soon, however, that, for lack of necessary preparation, the execution of the task did not fare as well as such an excellent theme demanded. I resolved therefore and promptly pledged myself to work out this right Royal theme more fully . . .

Your Majesty's most humble servant, the Author (J. S. BACH)

Translation from *The Bach Reader,* by H. T. David and A. Mendel, eds.

BEETHOVEN:

With Beethoven extemporization was . . . important. With paper before him he was one of the slowest and most laborious composers who ever lived, but with his fingers on the instrument he dashed away. His pupil Czerny says of him: "His improvisations were most beautiful and striking."   *Oxford Companion to Music*

Jahn says:

Beethoven, who was a youth of great promise came to Vienna in 1786, was taken to Mozart and at that musician's request played something for him which he, taking it for granted that it was a show-piece prepared for the occasion, praised in a rather cool manner. Beethoven observing this, begged Mozart to give him a theme for improvisation. He always played admirably when excited and now he was inspired, too, by the presence of the master whom he reverenced greatly; he played in such a style that Mozart, whose attention and interest grew more and more, finally said, "Keep your eyes on him; someday he will give the world something to talk about."

Czerny says:

In the mixed genre where, in the potpourri style, one thought follows upon another, as in his (Beethoven's) solo Fantasia, Op. 77. Often a few tones would suffice to enable him to improvise an entire piece (as, for instance, the Finale of the third Sonata, D major of Op. 10) . . . In teaching he laid great stress on the correct position of the fingers (after the School of Emanuel Bach, which he used in teaching me) . . .

The Life of Ludwig van Beethoven, by ALEXANDER THAYER

CASALS:

Count de Morphy, a pupil of Fetis and a personal friend of Gevaert, the famous Belgian musicologist. "At court he was known as *El Musico* . . . Every day . . . he used to ask me [Casals] to a drawing-room and make me improvise at the piano. In those days I was attracted by unusual harmonies, but when the Count, who sat next to me, thought I was going too far, he would tap me on the shoulder, saying, 'Pablito, do keep to more common language.' It was the period of *fin de siecle,* when extravagance was the fashion."

Conversations with Casals by J. MA. CORREDOR

LISZT ON Chopin:

His grand Polonaise in F sharp minor must be classed amongst his most energetic writings; and in it he has put a Mazurka. . . . The whole production is one of great originality, and excites us like the story of some broken dream told after a night of restless wakefulness in the first dull gray, cold, of a winter sunrise. It is a dream poem in which impressions and objects follow each other with startling incoherence and with the wildest transitions. . . . The chief motif is a weird air, as dark as the hour before a hurricane, when we catch the fierce exclamation of exasperation mingled with bold defiance recklessly hurled at the stormy elements. . . .

In the works of the great masters we know of nothing analogous to the striking effect produced by this passage, which is suddenly interrupted by a scene champetre, a Mazurka in the style of an idyl . . . but which, so far from effacing the memory of the bitter grief which has gone before, serves by its bitter irony of contrast to augment our painful emotions to such a degree that we feel almost a sensation of comfort at the return of the original phrase, and now, freed from the contradiction of a naive, simple, and inglorious happiness, we can once more sympathise with the noble yet fatal struggle. This Improvisation ends like a dream, with no other conclusion than a sort of convulsive shudder, and leaves the soul the subject of the strangest, wildest, and most subduing impressions.

Life of Chopin, by FRANZ LISZT

HUNEKER ON Liszt:

He [Liszt] introduced into the musty academic atmosphere of musical Europe a strong, fresh breeze from the Hungarian (puzta); this wandering pianoplayer of Hungarian-Austrian blood, a genuine cosmopolite, taught music a new charm, the charm of the unexpected, the improvised. The freedom of Beethoven in his later works and of Chopin in all his music, became the principal factor in the style of Liszt. Music must have the shape of an improvisation. In Hungarian rhapsodies, the majority of which begin in a mosque, and end in a tavern, are the extremes of his system.

Apart from his invention of a new form or, rather, the condensation and revisal of an old one, the symphonic poem—Liszt's greatest contribution to art—is the wild truant, rhapsodic, extempore element he infused into modern music; nature in her most reckless, untrammelled moods he interpreted with fidelity.　　*Franz Liszt* by JAMES HUNEKER

Confucius (551–478 B.C.) enunciated the teaching that all affairs of state should be regulated by music and ritual: music to order man's inner spirit, ritual and ceremony to regulate his outward behavior.　　*International Cyclopedia of Music and Musicians*

Rousseau in his Dictionary of Music (1767) actually defines "Fantaisie," a piece of instrumental music that one performs as one composes it. And he adds that a "Fantaisie" can never be written, because "as soon as it is written or repeated, it ceases to be a 'Fantaisie' and becomes an ordinary piece."　　*Oxford Companion to Music*

BARTÓK ON Folk Music:

In my studies of folk-music . . . I felt an urge . . . to collect and study Hungarian peasant music unknown until then. It was my great good luck to find a helpmate for this work in Zoltán Kodály. . . .

The outcome of these studies was of decisive influence upon my work, because it freed me from the tyrannical rule of the major and minor keys. The greater part of the collected treasure, and the more valuable part, was in old ecclesiastical or old Greek modes, or based on more primitive (pentatonic) scales, and the melodies were full of most free and varied rhythmic phrases and changes of tempi, played both *rubato* and *giusto*. It became clear to me that the old modes, which had been forgotten in our music, had lost nothing of their vigour. Their new employment made new rhythmic combinations possible. This new way of using the diatonic scale brought freedom from the rigid use of the major and minor keys, and eventually led to a new conception of the chromatic scale, every tone of which came to be considered of equal value and could be used freely and independently.

. . . At this point I have to mention a strange notion widespread some thirty or forty years ago. Most trained and good musicians then believed that only simple harmonizations were well suited to folk-tunes.

What kind of folk-songs did these musicians know? Mostly new German and Western songs and so-called folk-songs made up by popular composers. The melody of such songs usually moves along the triad of tonic and dominant; the main melody consists of a breaking up of these chords into single notes ("Oh Du lieber Augustin"). It is obvious that melodies of this description do not go well with a more complex harmonization.

But our musicians wanted to apply the theory derived from this type of song to an entirely different type of Hungarian songs built up on "pentatonic" scales.

It may sound odd, but I do not hesitate to say: the simpler the melody the more complex and strange may be the harmonization and accompaniment that go well with it. Let us for instance take a melody that moves on two successive notes only (there are many such melodies in Arab peasant music). It is obvious that we are much freer in the invention of an accompaniment than in the case of a melody of a more complex character. These primitive melodies, moreover, show no trace of the stereotyped joining of triads. That again means greater freedom for us in the treatment of the melody. It allows us to bring out the melody most clearly by building round it harmonies of the widest range varying along different keynotes. I might almost say that the traces of polytonality in modern Hungarian music and in Stravinsky's music are to be explained by this possibility.

Of his experiences in collecting folk songs in Turkey, Bartók wrote:

"He (of whom we learned later that he was a member of Parliament) called together a big gathering, invited two musicians from a neighboring village, and the people began dancing. And what a dance this was! The music was strange, almost frightening. One of the musicians played an instrument, called 'zurna,' which was a kind of oboe of very sharp tones; the other had a big drum, called 'devul,' slung over his shoulder. He beat his drum, using a wooden stick, with a diabolical fierceness, so that I expected that either his drum or my ear drums would split any moment. Even the flame of our oil lamp, flickering so peacefully, leapt high at every beat! And the dance! Four men performed it, one as a 'solo dancer,' the other three linked together, accompanying him with a few scanty movements only. At intervals the musicians, too, entered the dance with accompanying steps and movements. All of a sudden the music came to an end, the dancing stopped and a song broke forth. One of the three accompanying men had started singing, sunk in himself with an expression of devotion that I cannot describe in words. He started the song on the highest note of his high tenor voice and moved slowly downwards, as the song neared its end, to more human spheres.   *A Memorial Review,* published by Boosey & Hawkes

CHARLES IVES:

About the modern composer Charles Ives: "He wrote microtonal music, music in which liberty is left to individual players to follow their own feelings and even almost to extemporize portions. To represent multiplicity of American moods, Ives often introduced a free counterpoint on national tunes taken at different tempi and played in different keys. The improvisational element is also inherent in Ives' writing when one instrument is given a repeated refrain such as fiddlers employ in folk dances.

Oxford Companion to Music

Division, i.e., extempore variations on the viol:

A Ground, subject, or bass, (call it what you please) is pricked down in several papers; one for him who is to play the ground upon an organ, harpsichord, or whatever other instrument may be apt for that purpose; the other for him that plays upon the viol, who having the said ground before his eye as his theme or subject plays such variety of descant or division in concordance thereto as his skill and present invention do then suggest unto him. In this manner of play, which is the perfection of the viol or any other instrument, if it be exactly performed, a man may show the excellency both of his hand and invention, to the delight and admiration of those that hear him.

On Division Viol (1659) by CHRISTOPHER SIMPSON
in *Oxford Companion to Music*

. . . to the Jazz musician *How High the Moon* is not simply the melody . . . that can be found on the sheet music, but a harmonic ski-trail along which ten thousand musicians have travelled. (The improvisational bases of jazz are not melodies but chord structures. . . . Thus the uninitiated listeners . . . must be instructed in following the new melody created by the jazzman, based not on the missing melody the listener is seeking, but on a harmonic routine identical with that of the unplayed tune.)

The Book of Jazz, by LEONARD FEATHER

A Hint from Another Art:

Nowadays a round spot in a painting can be more significant than a human figure. A vertical line combined with a horizontal produce a sound that is almost dramatic. The impact of the acute angle of a triangle on a circle produces an effect no less powerful than the finger of God touching the finger of Adam in Michelangelo. And if fingers are not just anatomical or physiological but something more, so also a triangle or a circle is something more than geometry.

WASSILY KANDINSKY

Improvisation in Italy:

Neither the extended bibliographies of printed compositions nor the bulk of unpublished scores piled up in Italian, European and American libraries give a complete idea of the general diffusion and profound influence of music in Italian life after the spiritual and political revolution of the sixteenth century.

An even more eloquent expression of that almost delirious musical fervor is offered by the protracted vogue of vocal and instrumental improvisation. It became so popular as to represent a national habit, and not in music alone. For two centuries that sort of artistic and intellectual pastime was the typical and universal form of higher entertainment in all classes of Italian society, with poets, musicians, and even painters and comedians gaining frenzied public acclaim similar to that enjoyed in our day by boxing champions and motion-picture actors. In that era of Italian civilization the improvisation of verses and music was a common feature of social life.

The Genius of Italy, by LEONARDO OLSCHKI

Master-Drum Variations in African Music:

Playing variations is the main occupation of the master drummer when there is dancing. . . . The full flower of the music is in the variations of which the standard pattern is the nucleus. The musical technique is this: The master announces a standard pattern and repeats it several times to establish it. Now each standard pattern consists of several phrases or sentences. Any one of these can serve as a nucleus for variations. But the first phrase is all-important. It is the SEED of the pattern. The whole standard pattern grows out of this seed. So also do the variations on that pattern. Thus, after establishing a standard pattern, the master drummer, by extension, simile, or any other artifice at his command, using the first phrase as a germinal idea, builds up spontaneously a series of variations which continue as long as the inspiration of that particular phrase lasts. Having started with this "seed," as Tay puts it, the master drummer can go anywhere he likes, for everyone will know that your plant has grown from this seed. Normally you cannot start variations by improvising on, say, section B or section C of a standard pattern. Some drummers might do this, but sooner or later they *must* introduce the "seed" which is section A. The worst course is to start your variations on some part of the standard pattern other than section A and then go on without bringing in the seed at all. Mr. Tay says this will be "just playing in the air without any background. People would hardly know on what pattern you were playing variations."

Studies in African Music, by the REV. A. M. JONES

Oriental Music:

Oriental music, whether Semitic, Altaic, or Hindu, is based on the model form.

A mode (in Arabic and Persian: Makam or Naghana) is composed of a number of motives (i.e., short music figures or groups of tones) within a certain scale. The motives have different functions. There are beginning and concluding motives, and motives of conjunctive and disjunctive character. The composer operates with the material of these traditional folk motives within a certain mode for his creations. His composition is nothing but his arrangement and combination of these limited number of motives. His "freedom" of creation consists further in embellishments and in modulations from one mode to the other.

The next element is the emphasis upon ornament. Oriental music is unthinkable in long sustained notes. On the contrary it is of a vivid tonal character. Either a note is short, or if long, it quavers in a tremolo and is adorned with ornaments.

The Oriental musicians and laymen are fond of improvisation. Even set tunes are largely varied and modified. The improvisation occurs in a certain mode, and the improviser has to operate with the traditional motive therein.

Oriental music is without any harmony. The only beauty the Oriental finds is in the melodic line and in the intricate ornamentation. Occasionally in unison singing of a group there are fourths or fifths, due solely to the range of the voices, but not to harmonic instincts, because the people sing frequently in seconds or in any other "discord."

Jewish Music, by A. Z. IDELSOHN

Music in India:

Many who would not witness a dance program will sit, with no loss of respectability, enthralled by the hour as some singer surrounded by three or four musicians spins out his melodies. . . . Dance programs list the scale in which the melodies are sung (raga) and the meter (tala) of the composition as if for a music program. The effect of South Indian music is ecstatic and exuberant. It is probably the happiest, most released music in the world.

. . . Music begins . . . Within the rigid rules controlling fractional entries on ¼ and ¹⁄₁₆ beats, and working within the minute, twenty-two purely tempered, tonal divisions (srutis) of the Indian octave, they abandon themselves to a mood of ecstasy. In joyous release the singer shouts his song and the drummer forces his rhythms out of his hide-and-wood instrument. Together, they bend their bodies, shake their heads in approbation (although the gesture looks to Westerners as if they are saying "no, no"), and apparently remain seated with difficulty as they bring out their music. The singer is the core of the music, the drummer, music's life. The drummer and singer focus their attention on each other with a svengali-like intensity. Each seems to draw out of the other effort upon effort, precision upon precision, perfection upon perfection, until each passage is drained of further possibilities, improvisations, or nuances. This is the music the Bharata Natya dancer borrows, and in borrowing has selected only the most beautiful to incorporate into dance.

Three types of singing, determined by the nature of the dancer, are performed in Bharata Natya:
1. Ordinary poetic songs with words.
2. Songs without words, but sung in the Indian Solfeggio system (comparable to our do-re-mi) for those portions of dance in which the melody of the raga is important, called svara. This sometimes is a tonal exposition of the melody which will be followed by the words of the song in exactly the same tonal pattern. Svara may also be an independent melodic line having no reference to a subsequent song with words. Svara is designed to exhibit melody unhindered by word or meaning. By its solfeggio an added virtuosity, that of speed in syllable pronunciation, appears.
3. Songs (if they can so be called) without melody or words, called sollukkatu. These are . . . rhythmic chants whose syllables dictate the complex meters of dance passages.

The Dance in India, by FAUBION BOWERS

Music [in India] is thought to intrude if it tries to imitate or duplicate the emotions of an actor and his words. At best it burnishes. At most it adds only repose and agitation, quiet or exuberance.

When you approach Asian music you must wipe from your mind your ear's preconditioning by harmony and the forms you associate with musical structure in the West. You must listen for the infinite melodic variations, the subtle contortions of the basic theme, the gossamer-fine tonal web of clear, thin pitch, and the formality of progressing from the simple to the complex, from the slow to the fast, or for the introspective, thoughtful strumming when the musician plays with after-resonance, vibration, or the contemplative setting of mood.

In principle it works out this way. Always there is a steady drone bass or a single tonic which serves as a backdrop to enhance the tonal variation. Over this the melodic differentiations waver like spun thread. Against it sounds the intricate rhythmic patterns.

The music in India and Southeast Asia, with the exception of Bali, is nearly always improvisatory, the creation of the performing musician in that moment and almost never the interpretive rendering of another's recorded composition. With the exceptions of Thailand, Cambodia, Java and again Bali, no music in Asia is continuously chordal, orchestral, or even contrapuntal, and the harmonic development even here is mostly one of accident and the collision of the several instrumental melodies. While to the Westerner this may appear as a deficiency, to the Asian our vast orchestras and the ubiquitous piano have only deadened our ears to his more exact tunings and more subtle metres. Where one is finely melodic, the other is richly harmonic. Where one depends on drums, and their infinite possibilities of rhythmic intricacy, the other sacrifices this for a broader coordination and variety of timbres. Altogether, the technical and aesthetic differences between Asian and Western music are hard to resolve . . . If the student of Asian dance and drama is to arrive at full understanding, he must make his greatest effort on music. It must be listened to with the mind without reference to his own conventions. He must try, despite the handicap of inexperience, to catch the microtonic tonal divisions and the elusive pulsating rhythms. At the end, finally, familiarity will allow the unconscious and relaxed attitude which indulges the emotions.

The rewards are great. Emotionally, it is as affecting and inspiring—in different ways and in different areas of aesthetic sensibility—as our own. And certainly Asian music extends our preconceptions of the theory of music into reaches scarcely imagined before by us. Its delights and pleasures, once the fundamentals are grasped, are quite as profoundly gratifying as the more immediately accessible dances and dramas.

Theatre in the East, by FAUBION BOWERS

Selected Bibliography

BARLOW, H., and MORGENSTERN, S. *Dictionary of Musical Themes*. New York: Crown Publishers, 1948.

BOWERS, FAUBION. *The Dance in India*. New York: Columbia University Press, 1953.

BOWERS, FAUBION. *Theatre in the East, A Survey of Asian Dance and Drama*. New York: Grove Press, 1960.

BRITTEN, B., and HOLST, I. *The Wonderful World of Music*. New York: Doubleday & Co., 1958.

DORIAN, FREDERICK. *The Musical Workshop*. New York: Harper & Brothers, 1947.

DOWLING, LYLE, and SHAW, ARNOLD (eds.). *Schillinger System of Musical Composition*. New York: Carl Fischer, 1946.

FELLERER, K. G. (ed.). *Anthology of Music* (in English), vol. 12. Cologne: Arno Volk Verlag. Sole selling agent, Leeds Music Corp., New York.

FERAND, ERNEST. *Die Improvisation in der Musik*. Zurich: Rhein Verlag, 1938.

FERAND, ERNEST. *Improvisation in Nine Centuries of Western Music*, vol. 12. Fellerer, K. G. (ed.) Anthology of Music (in English). Cologne: Arne Volk Verlag. Sole selling agent, Leeds Music Corp. New York.

JAQUES-DALCROZE, ÉMILE. *Eurythmics*. London: Novello & Co., Ltd., 1920.

JONES, ARTHUR MORRIS. *Studies in African Music*. New York: Oxford University Press, 1959.

MOREUX, SERGE. *Béla Bartók* (translated from the French by G. S. Fraser and Erik de Mauny.) London: The Harvill Press, Ltd., 1953.

RETI, RUDOLPH R. *Thematic Process in Music*. London: Faber & Faber, Ltd., 1961.

RUFER, JUSEF. *Composition with Twelve Tones Related Only to One Another* (translated by Humphrey Searle). New York: The Macmillan Co., 1954.

SCHLIEDER, FREDERICK W. *Lyric Composition Through Improvisation*. Boston: C. C. Birchard & Co., 1927.

SCHOLES, PERCY ALFRED. *Oxford Companion to Music*. New York: Oxford University Press, 1955.

SEEGER, RUTH CRAWFORD. *American Folk Songs for Children*. New York: Doubleday & Co., 1948.

SLONIMSKY, NICOLAS. *Thesaurus of Scales and Melodic Patterns*. New York: Coleman-Ross Co., 1947.

INDEX

187

188